Blue Star

The Story of Corabelle Fellows
Teacher at Dakota Missions
1884–1888

KUNIGUNDE DUNCAN
With a New Introduction by
BRUCE DAVID FORBES

D1569157

MINNESOTA HISTORICAL SOCIETY PRESS
ST. PAUL · 1990

Borealis Books are high-quality paperback reprints of books chosen by the Minnesota Historical Society Press for their importance as enduring historical sources and their value as enjoyable accounts of life in the Upper Midwest.

∞ The paper used in this publication meets the minimum requirements of the American National Standard for Information Sciences—Permanence for Printed Library Materials, ANSI Z39.48–1984.

Minnesota Historical Society Press, St. Paul 55101
First published 1938 by The Caxton Printers, Ltd., Caldwell, Idaho
New material copyright 1990 by the Minnesota Historical Society

International Standard Book Number 0-87351-245-6
Manufactured in the United States of America
10 9 8 7 6 5 4 3 2 1

Library of Congress Cataloging-in-Publication Data
Duncan, Kunigunde, 1886-
    Blue star : the story of Corabelle Fellows, teacher at Dakota Missions, 1884-1888 / Kunigunde Duncan; with a new introduction by Bruce David Forbes.
        p.   cm.
    Reprint. Originally published: Caldwell, Idaho : Caxton Printers, 1938.
    ISBN 0-87351-245-6 (alk. paper)
    1. Fellows, Corabelle. 2. Dakota Indians—Education. 3. Teachers—South Dakota—Biography. 4. Dakota Indians—Missions. 5. Dakota Indians—Social life and customs. 6. Rosebud Indian Reservation (S.D.) 7. Cheyenne River Indian Reservation (S.D.)
    l. Title.
E97.65.S8F453   1990   89-39848
306'.0899750783—dc20   CIP

Blue Star

"I remember just as well as if it were yesterday how–"

TO INDIAN WOMEN

C O N T E N T S

ILLUSTRATIONS

INTRODUCTION
TO THE
REPRINT EDITION

*B*LUE STAR is a volume of reminiscences that portrays Indian life as observed by a non-Indian teacher who lived among them. That teacher, Corabelle Fellows, told her story about life with the Dakota and Lakota people from 1884 to 1888 to free-lance writer Kunigunde Duncan. Fellows described native culture, but most of what she said came through her own cultural filter. More than a description of Indian culture, the book is a case study of a white teacher among Native Americans. What motivated her and other whites to leave their homes and familiar surroundings to teach among Native Americans? What did they intend to accomplish? What attitudes did they carry about Indians, the relative worth of cultures, and the value of what they were doing? From one teacher's personal recollections come answers, and it is in this area that the book is most valuable.[1]

In works on Indian-white relations, one usually learns more about the white side of the encounter, especially when the author is non-Indian, and when most of the traditional written evidence is by non-Indians. This book is no excep-

[1] I am especially thankful to Phyllis White Shield Gough, Sicangu Lakota (Rosebud Sioux); Elizabeth Riggs Gutch, chair of the Historical Committee of the United Church of Christ in South Dakota; Sarah Rubinstein, editor of Borealis Books for the Minnesota Historical Society Press; Jane Kolbe, director of the South Dakota State Library; and Linda Sommer, director of the South Dakota State Archives, for assistance, helpful comments, and insights in the preparation of this introduction.

tion. Yet Native Americans were full participants in the exchange, with their own historical traditions and cultural understandings, offering their own initiatives and evaluations.

When Europeans arrived in North America, more than two hundred markedly distinct cultures existed on the continent. Various tribal groups spoke mutually unintelligible languages (not just dialects) and had entirely different forms of housing, food, and religious beliefs and practices. While some generalizations about their cultures may apply, the differences are far more numerous. Yet non-Indians frequently overgeneralize about Native Americans, and when they do, the stereotypical image is of a nomadic Plains warrior, with a flowing headdress, on horseback, hunting buffalo, living in a tepee. The image, shaped by western movies and a popular interest in Indian-white military conflicts that took place on the northern plains from the 1850s to 1890, derives many of its aspects from the Sioux people, the very people with whom Fellows worked. Fellows did not work with Indians in general; she worked with a particular nation of people, who often were linked to popular stereotypes.

In designating this particular group, there are problems with the widely used term Sioux. The word has a derogatory connotation because it is a shortened form of the word French explorers heard the Ojibway use to describe their rival neighbors. The French wrote down the sounds they heard as "nadouessioux" or variant spellings; Sioux became the shortened form. The original Ojibway term meant snakes, adders, or, in other words, enemies. In their own language the people call themselves Dakota (or Lakota and Nakota in dialects), which means friends or allies. Because of dialect differences among subgroups, many historians and anthropologists have struggled to find an appropriate umbrella term for the subgroups, and many still resort to Sioux as the best alternative.

In the mid-seventeenth century, when first encountered by Europeans, the people called the Sioux lived west of the Great Lakes, primarily in present-day central and southern

Minnesota. They referred to themselves as the Seven Council
Fires or Seven Fireplaces (Oceti Sakowin), which referred
to their subdivisions of social and political organization—
Mdewakanton, Wahpeton, Sisseton, Wahpekute, Yankton,
Yanktonai, and Teton. By the middle of the next century,
partially under pressure from the Ojibway to the north, they
moved south and west, remaining in southern Minnesota and
moving into what is now South Dakota.

In the process three cultural clusters developed. The
Mdewakanton, Wahpeton, Sisseton, and Wahpekute remained in southern Minnesota, lived near rivers or lakes,
retained many cultural features of the eastern woodlands,
and spoke the Dakota dialect. They are called, collectively,
eastern Sioux, Dakota, or Santee (from Isanti, people of the
Knife Lake—perhaps referring to Mille Lacs). The Yankton
and Yanktonai settled in what is now eastern South Dakota
and became known as the middle Sioux or Nakota. The
Teton were the largest of the Seven Council Fires, large
enough to have seven council fires of their own as subdivisions (Oglala, Brule, Hunkpapa, Minneconjou, Blackfoot,
Two Kettles, and Sans Arcs). Living in what is now mostly
western South Dakota, they adopted characteristics of
nomadic Plains tribes and relied on the horse and buffalo.
Their dialect and self-designation is Lakota, and they are also
called Teton or western Sioux. Fellows worked at first with
the Dakota and later with the Lakota people.[2]

Each group had been pushed into jarring cultural transi-
tions prior to Fellows's arrival. The Dakota people had lost

[2] Information about Sioux or Dakota/Lakota nomenclature, classifica-
tions, and culture can be found in many sources. Examples include James
H. Howard, "The Cultural Position of the Dakota: A Reassessment," in *Essays
in the Science of Culture in Honor of Leslie A. White,* ed. G. Dole and R.
Carneiro (New York: Thomas Y. Crowell Co., 1960), 250–57; Alanson B.
Skinner, "A Sketch of Eastern Dakota Ethnology," *American Anthropologist*
21 (1919): 164–74; William K. Powers, *Oglala Religion* (Lincoln: University of Nebraska Press, 1977), 3–24; Royal B. Hassrick, *The Sioux* (Norman:
University of Oklahoma Press, 1964), 4–7.

xiv INTRODUCTION

most of their land in Minnesota through treaties in 1837, 1851, and 1858.[3] After 1851 they were restricted, at least in theory, to land along both sides of the Minnesota River, about 140 miles long and 20 miles wide. In 1858 they lost the northern half of the reserve. Unable in this limited area to maintain their traditional life-style, they were encouraged by missionaries and government agents to adopt many features of white culture. Big Eagle, a Dakota leader whose reminiscences are widely quoted, complained that

> the whites were always trying to make the Indians give up their life and live like white men—go to farming, work hard and do as they did—and the Indians did not know how to do that, and did not want to anyway. It seemed too sudden to make such a change. If the Indians had tried to make the whites live like them, the whites would have resisted, and it was the same way with many Indians.[4]

A whole list of causes, including pressure for cultural change, led to the Dakota War of 1862, also called the Dakota Conflict or the Sioux Uprising. Crushed quickly, the war engendered such intense indiscriminate white bitterness against all Dakota people that most surviving Dakota Indians who did not flee to the West or Canada were imprisoned and herded out of Minnesota. In 1866 many of the Santee settled near the junction of the Niobrara and Missouri rivers in northeastern Nebraska Territory. By 1869 the federal government designated a small rectangle of land there, about

[3] Roy W. Meyer, *History of the Santee Sioux: United States Indian Policy on Trial* (Lincoln: University of Nebraska Press, 1967), 24–108; Charles J. Kappler, comp. and ed., *Indian Affairs, Laws and Treaties* (Washington, D.C.: Government Printing Office, 1904), 2:588–93.
[4] Jerome Big Eagle, "A Sioux Story of the War," *Collections of the Minnesota Historical Society* 6 (1894): 382–400, reprinted in Gary Clayton Anderson and Alan R. Woolworth, eds., *Through Dakota Eyes: Narrative Accounts of the Minnesota Indian War of 1862* (St. Paul: Minnesota Historical Society Press, 1988), 23.

twelve by fifteen miles, as the Santee Reservation.[5] A year
later missionary Alfred Riggs established a boarding school
at this location. Corabelle Fellows arrived at this school in
1884 for her first teaching assignment among Indians. The
Dakota people she met had been removed from their
homeland for two decades but had suffered ongoing cultural
and geographic disruption for many years preceding.

The Lakota, with a homeland farther west, had faced such
turmoil more recently. The Fort Laramie Treaty of 1868
established a Great Sioux Reservation that encompassed most
of what is now western South Dakota plus surrounding territory. The Sioux Agreement of 1877 reduced the Great
Sioux Reservation from approximately 60 million to less than
22 million acres, and another Sioux Agreement in 1889
reduced it further, to the boundaries of the Cheyenne River,
Crow Creek, Lower Brule, Pine Ridge, Rosebud, and Standing Rock reservations. Between 1858 and 1889, through a
process of questionable legality, the Teton, Yankton, and
Yanktonai had relinquished 81.7 percent of their land.[6] A
gold rush in the Black Hills and white interest in ranchland
had spurred the takeover, but relatively few whites actually settled in the vast dry terrain of western South Dakota.
Thus, while the Lakota found themselves restricted, they
were not surrounded by the same kind of concentrated
white presence as the Dakota were. They experienced ongoing military conflict on the northern plains, however, which
culminated in the 1890 massacre at Wounded Knee.

Government agents and missionaries actively promoted
cultural change among the Lakota—an unpromising under-
taking. Charles McChesney, the Indian agent at the Cheyenne
River Agency, complained in 1887 about the "drawbacks

[5] Meyer, *History of the Santee Sioux,* 155–74; Kappler, comp. and ed.,
Indian Affairs, 1:861–64; Roy W. Meyer, "The Establishment of the Santee
Reservation, 1866–1869," *Nebraska History* 45 (March 1964): 59–97.
[6] Herbert T. Hoover, "The Sioux Agreement of 1889 and Its After-
math," *South Dakota History* 19 (Spring 1989): 58–59.

to successful agriculture" in the region and questioned the government's attempt to promote crop raising:

> Since about 1872 efforts have been put forth by every agent to make agriculturalists of these Indians, but the soil and climate will not allow it. . . . It may be said that the Indian has been furnished with an occupation to employ his time; but I see no good in keeping these Indians employed at what they can not make a living at in this country.[7]

McChesney recommended redirecting efforts toward the care of stock. Besides encouraging agriculture and stock raising, the other major government activity was educating Indian children in day and boarding schools. These schools, alongside mission schools, engaged in an active program of acculturation. When Agent McChesney attempted to assess the "steady, stable advancement" of the people at Cheyenne River, these are the "evidences" he listed: interest in the English language, monogamy replacing polygamy, desire for stock, building houses and asking for floors in them, and discarding "the clothing of their ancient custom" and wearing "that of the white man."[8]

The text of *Blue Star* provides many anecdotes and general descriptions, but it is surprisingly vague about some accompanying data the reader might expect: specific dates and full names of people and institutions. It is likely that the free-lance writer to whom Fellows told her story filtered out some details as irrelevant for the general reader. From outside sources, however, we can fill in some missing pieces.

Fellows left her home in Washington, D.C., on November 20, 1884, and arrived at the Santee Reservation on the day

---

[7] United States Office of Indian Affairs, *Annual Report, 1887,* 17 (hereafter cited as OIA, *Annual Report*).

[8] OIA, *Annual Report, 1888,* 28.

before Thanksgiving to teach at a mission school.⁹ While
the formal name of the school and the first names of her
host and hostess are not provided in the book, they are easily
identified as the Santee Normal Training School, admin-
istered by Alfred Longley and Mary Buel Riggs.

The school's origins were rooted in southern Minnesota
missionary efforts that the American Board of Commis-
sioners for Foreign Missions (ABCFM) began among the
Dakota people in 1834. The ABCFM was a cooperative
Presbyterian-Congregational agency and sponsored the most
substantial missionary force in southern Minnesota in the
next thirty years. Two of the prominent ABCFM missionaries
in the period were Thomas S. Williamson and Stephen
Return Riggs, both of whose children continued their
parents' work. The missionaries' major accomplishment was
linguistic, with much energy spent reducing the Dakota
language to writing, compiling dictionaries, producing a
spelling book, and translating the Bible and other "spiritual
literature." They encouraged domestic agriculture, opened
schools, and sought converts to Christianity. Yet, after
almost thirty years of work, Thomas Williamson could
report only fifty-two full-blood and fifteen mixed-blood
Dakota members of ABCFM mission churches on the eve of
the Dakota War of 1862. After the war, missionaries continued their work with the Dakota through the period of
the Indians' imprisonment and relocation. Wholesale con-
versions, numbering in the hundreds, followed. What missionaries saw as God's reward for their long, sacrificial labor,
most anthropologists explain as a result of cultural disruption, wherein persons in turmoil look for a new organizing
center for their lives.¹⁰

⁹ Corabelle Fellows, "Views of a New Teacher," *The Word Carrier,*
January 1885, p. 3, "My Sewing Class," *The Word Carrier,* August-September
1885, p. 1.
¹⁰ Bruce David Forbes, "Evangelization and Acculturation Among the
Santee Dakota Indians, 1834–1864" (Ph.D. diss., Princeton Theological
Seminary, 1977), especially chapter 2; Stephen R. Riggs, *Mary and I: Forty*

As the Dakota were resettled farther west, Thomas Williamson and Stephen Riggs continued some activity among them, but their children became the resident missionaries. John P. Williamson worked with the Santee until 1869 and then moved to nearby Greenwood, South Dakota, to minister to the Yankton until his death in 1917.[11] Stephen and Mary Riggs had eight children, at least four of whom devoted their lives to missionary service.[12] Alfred Longley Riggs (1837-1916), the eldest son, founded the Santee Normal Training School on the Santee Reservation in 1870. In 1871 the Presbyterians withdrew from the interdenominational ABCFM to work under their own Presbyterian Board of Missions, and the Williamsons were taken under care of the Presbyterian board. Stephen Riggs, although a Presbyterian, chose to stay with the ABCFM, and his sons became Congregational ministers as the missionary work was separated between the two denominations. Yet, although a formal division between denominations occurred, in the Dakota field cooperation continued. As an example, the Dakota-English mission newspaper *Iapi Oaye: The Word Carrier* was founded in 1871, and for much of its history the Presbyterian John Williamson edited the Dakota portion while the Congregationalist Alfred Riggs edited the English.[13] Considering this back-

Years with the Sioux (Chicago: W. G. Holmes, 1880); Stephen R. Riggs, *Tahkoo Wah-kan: or, the Gospel among the Dakotas* (Boston: Congregation Sabbath-school and Publishing Society, 1869); Jon Willand, *Lac Qui Parle and the Dakota Mission* (Madison, Minn.: Lac qui Parle County Historical Society, 1964).

[11] Winifred W. Barton, *John P. Williamson: A Brother to the Sioux* (New York: Fleming H. Revell Co., 1919).

[12] Henry Earle Riggs, *Our Pioneer Ancestors: Being a record of available information as to the Riggs, Baldridge, Agnew, Earle, Kirkpatrick, Vreeland and allied families* (Ann Arbor, Mich.: Edwards Brothers, Inc., 1942), 61–66.

[13] Founded in 1871 as a bilingual newspaper, in 1884 it separated into two editions, with *Iapi Oaye* as the name of the Dakota paper and *The Word Carrier* as the name of the English one. Even in separate editions, the cooperation continued. Beginning in 1887 both newspapers were printed on Santee Normal's own printing press.

ground, it is not surprising that a Presbyterian church sent Corabelle Fellows to work in a Congregational school (p. 56).

By the time Corabelle Fellows arrived, Santee Normal included eighteen buildings on 480 acres and counted 206 students in its boarding school, day school, and some auxiliary activities. The boarding school was the heart of the enterprise, emphasizing religious instruction and industrial training. Prayers were a regular part of daily life, and attendance at church and Sunday school was mandatory. One teacher claimed that "it is an exception when any pupil goes thru the school without becoming a Christian." Industrial training involved farming, carpentry, printing, and blacksmith arts for boys and sewing, cooking, and housekeeping for girls. Traditional Euro-American subjects such as arithmetic, geography, history, drawing, music, reading, writing, composition, and physiology were also part of the curriculum.[14]

The school provided training in reading and writing the Dakota language although there were specific times when only English could be spoken. The mission tradition out of which the school arose had invested much in the vernacular, and ABCFM leaders believed that it was the most effective approach for generating interest both in education and in Christianity. When a federal directive in 1887 insisted that all instruction in government and mission schools be solely in English, Alfred Riggs refused to comply. He mobilized opposition and editorialized repeatedly in *The Word Carrier:* "These rules are clearly ILLEGAL, UNSCIENTIFIC, IRRELIGIOUS, is the verdict which will ultimately be given by the civilized and Christian portion of the United States."[15]

[14] Richard L. Guenther, "The Santee Normal Training School," *Nebraska History* 51 (Fall 1970), 359–78, reprinted as a pamphlet by the Nebraska State Historical Society; Mary B. Riggs, *Early Days at Santee: The Beginnings of Santee Normal Training School* (Santee, Nebr.: Santee N.T.S. Press, 1928).

[15] *The Word Carrier,* August-September 1887, p. 1. The July-December 1887 issues of *The Word Carrier* were filled with comments about the federal prohibition of the use of the vernacular in Indian schools.

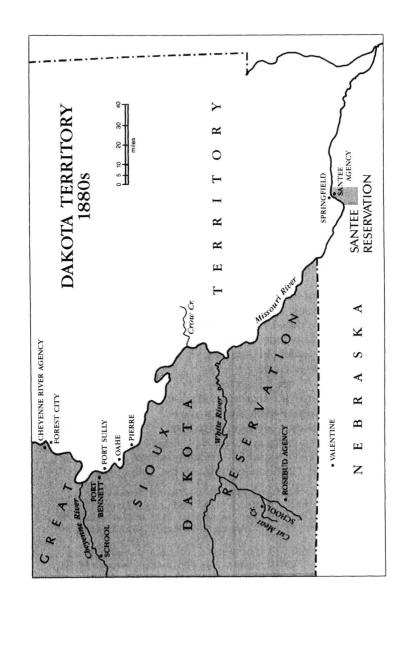

DAKOTA TERRITORY
1880s

miles
0 5 10 20 30 40

CHEYENNE RIVER AGENCY
• FOREST CITY

G R E A T

Cheyenne River

SCHOOL
FORT BENNETT •

• FORT SULLY
• OAHE
• PIERRE

S I O U X

D A K O T A

Crow Cr.

White River

R E S E R V A T I O N

Cut Meat Cr.
SCHOOL
• ROSEBUD AGENCY

Missouri River

T E R R I T O R Y

• VALENTINE

N E B R A S K A

SPRINGFIELD
SANTEE AGENCY

SANTEE
RESERVATION

Therefore, when Fellows mentioned that children were reprimanded for speaking Dakota (p. 69), it is misleading if it suggests that the mission school totally banned the Dakota language.

The language issue was important, for boarding schools represented a thoroughgoing attempt to immerse Indian children in a microcosm of white society, isolating them from traditional influences. Critics of a later time, who value pluralism, see such boarding schools as a prime example of cultural imperialism.[16] Santee Normal's investment in the Dakota language and interest in native leadership were the two major exceptions to this total program to supplant traditional culture. Beyond the two exceptions, Santee Normal attempted to inculcate white culture, values, and world views. The introduction of a cultural alternative was symbolized well in Corabelle Fellows's description—with all of its nuances and judgments—of the school soon after her arrival at Santee:

> This mission is a wonder to me, it is so neat, quiet and orderly. Everything that is done is like clockwork. And when I think of the one hundred and thirty-five pupils who attend this school, with their wild, free, youthful Indian spirits, I marvel more and more at the prompt obedience with which each pupil has an allotted task, performs it, not always quickly, but, as I have heard people say, very well *for an Indian*.[17]

Fellows came to Santee Normal to be trained. In announcing her arrival *The Word Carrier* said that "she will assist in various capacities and at the same time be pursuing her

[16] See Robert F. Berkhofer, Jr., *Salvation and the Savage: An Analysis of Protestant Missions and American Indian Response, 1787–1862* (Lexington: University of Kentucky Press, 1965), chapter 2, for a discussion of the cultural impact of day and boarding schools on Indian children.

[17] Corabelle Fellows, "Views of a New Teacher," *The Word Carrier*, January 1885, p. 3.

studies in the native language and become initiated into the practical part of mission work."[18] She taught Indian students arithmetic, reading, and sewing but expressed the hope that she might "not only be their teacher but their friend as well."[19]

In addition to her home Presbyterian church, the organization that officially sponsored her was the Woman's National Indian Association of Philadelphia. Alfred Riggs saw it as virtually an auxiliary of the male Indian Rights Association, which lobbied to abolish the reservation system. Riggs felt that the women's organization was out of its sphere when it attempted to be a missionary organization as well as a lobbying one. The association saw itself as a nondenominational organization that initiated missions and recruited missionaries but then turned them over to other bodies. Riggs felt that with no plan of mission and no sustained effort it only dabbled in activities for which it was unfit. Riggs's objections to the association did not prevent him from accepting Fellows at the school or from rooming with his family.[20]

After Fellows had been at Santee for seven months, she was transferred to a mission at Oahe on the Missouri River near Fort Sully. The missionary in charge there was Thomas Lawrence Riggs (1847-1940), Alfred's younger brother. He had been with Alfred at Santee Normal in the summer of 1870, helping with construction of the school. Two years later, after completing his seminary education, he established a mission on the upper Missouri, "in accord with Father's plan." He acknowledged that he relied greatly on "the wise advice and suggestions of my two 'elder brothers,' John and Alfred"; the Oahe mission seemed to be an extension of the missionary work by John Williamson at the Yankton Agen-

---

[18] *The Word Carrier,* November 1884, p. 1.
[19] "Mission Letter," *The Word Carrier,* August-September 1885, p. 2.
[20] *The Word Carrier,* October-December 1885, p. 1, February 1886, p. 3, March 1886, p. 2.

cy and the educational work by Alfred Riggs at Santee.[21]

The central station for Thomas Riggs's mission was Oahe, which by 1884-85 had a formal industrial school for Indian children. Yet equally significant was a network of thirteen out-stations he established on the nearby Cheyenne River Indian Reservation, providing one-room schools and centers for missionary activity. Thomas Riggs firmly believed in native leadership, claiming that "the Indian was a great deal more effective as a preacher and teacher among his own people than any white man could be."[22] To staff these out-stations he actively recruited Santee graduates. With other persons moving from Santee Normal to the Oahe mission, it was natural for Corabelle Fellows, although a non-Indian, to do so as well.

After spending a few months with the Thomas Riggs family at Oahe, Fellows was sent to a missionary out-station in the Oahenoupa village on the Cheyenne River, arriving there on October 21, 1885. Perhaps the most memorable person in Fellows's narrative is the woman with whom she lived at this station. Identified in the text only as Elizabeth, she was Elizabeth Winyan, whom Fellows described in a newspaper article as "an excellent Indian woman, the missionary for this station. She is nearly sixty years old, and there are few in these regions who do not know her, as she was among the first Christian Indians, and has lived with, and known the Riggs family for a good many years."[23] At least as told through Duncan, Fellows conveyed the impression that she

---

[21] Thomas Lawrence Riggs, "Sunset to Sunset: A Lifetime With My Brothers, the Dakotas," as told to his niece Margaret Kellogg Howard, *South Dakota Department of History Report and Historical Collections* 29 (1958), 87–306 (quotations on p. 111).

[22] Thomas Riggs, "Sunset to Sunset," 180. For a list of persons who came from Santee to work at the Oahe mission, see p. 181–82.

[23] Corabelle Fellows, "The Indian Problem," *The Word Carrier,* October-December 1885, p. 4. (The title of the article seems to be misstated, since it has nothing to do with the content.) Also see Fellows's description of Elizabeth Winyan in *The Word Carrier,* January 1886, p. 4.

was the official teacher, while Elizabeth was a sort of assistant who welcomed Fellows into her home and helped her adjust to local customs. In fact, the situation was the reverse. Elizabeth Winyan was the missionary in charge of the station and was the teacher in its one-room school. Fellows was *her* assistant. Winyan died in 1890 at Fort Bennett, praised by Thomas Riggs as his "Indian mother."[24]

Alfred Riggs had told Fellows she would be going among "rougher Indians," and at Elizabeth Winyan's out-station she certainly was among people less acculturated than those at Santee. A report written by Fellows and printed in *The Word Carrier* said, "I am living now in the 'Indian wilds,' sure enough. I am daily and hourly, you might say, surrounded by painted faces, and never a white person in sight for many, many miles."[25]

In Fellows's next assignment she was in charge of a government day school on the Cheyenne River Indian Reservation. Fellows said that in the spring the Indian agent wrote telling her to go "to another center," which she identified as Cut Meat Creek (p. 146, 147). The Indian Office annual report for 1887 listed her as an employee at an undesignated Cheyenne River Agency day school from April 1 to June 30, 1887.[26] The details of and reasons for her shift from a mission school to a government school are unclear, although we should not assume too much of a distinction between the two. For instance Fellows twice referred to William and Rebecca Holmes whom she identified as "a couple who served the Episcopal Church" (p. 184, 204), yet Indian Office reports identified them as employees at a government day school.[27] In 1887 the Cheyenne River Agency listed one government boarding school, eight government day schools, an Episcopal boarding school, and nine Congrega-

---

[24] *The Word Carrier*, February 1890, p. 1.
[25] *The Word Carrier*, October-December 1885, p. 4, January 1886, p. 2.
[26] OIA, *Annual Report, 1887*, 329.
[27] OIA, *Annual Report, 1888*, 391.

tional day schools under the direction of Thomas Riggs.[28] A major difference between the schools was the language used for instruction—only English in the government ones and the vernacular at the Riggs schools.

Fellows left Cut Meat Creek after her assistant fled, because "it was thought too risky for me to stay alone" (p. 178). After a midwestern speaking tour on behalf of Indians and a vacation in Iowa, she worked briefly at a boarding school at Fort Bennett where she met Samuel Campbell (also called Chaska or Chaska-Campbell), the son of a trader and a Sioux woman who was raised by the Episcopal priest at Fort Bennett after his mother's death. Fellows's final teaching assignment was at the Cheyenne River Agency's "No. 4 day school" on the Missouri River in Swift Bird's camp, about fifty-five miles northeast of the agency and, as Fellows noted, seventy-five miles from Fort Bennett (p. 183). The Indian Office report for 1888 recorded that she was employed at this day school until May 2, 1888.[29] She married Campbell on March 15, 1888, and gained some national notoriety thereby. The young couple soon accepted offers to go on a speaking tour (p. 204), and Corabelle Fellows's few years as a teacher among the Dakota and Lakota people came to an end.

The narrative concludes there, and information about Corabelle Fellows's life after 1888 is limited. About fifty years later, when Fellows was seventy-six years old and blind, she told her story to author Kunigunde Duncan. In a personal letter to Louisa (Mrs. Thomas) Riggs written in 1939 shortly after the publication of *Blue Star,* Duncan briefly described what she knew of Fellows's later life:

> Mrs. Tillman died an heroic death, smiling to the last, courteous, grateful for the least attention, after what seems to have been a very difficult life. Her

[28] OIA, *Annual Report, 1887,* 19.
[29] OIA, *Annual Report, 1888,* 391.

Indian husband left her for an Indian woman. She
made a living for her two small sons by writing and
teaching. After many years she met and married a
Civil War veteran who became the father of three
daughters. All of her children did well excepting the
eldest son who became a drunkard and a derelict.
She chose to remain with him, after Mr. Tillman's
death, because, as she said, he needed her love
most. He, however, abused her, mistreated her
shamelessly and, after her blindness, stole her one
means of support, her state blind pension. Thus she
was hungry most of the time, and always cold in
winter. I found her in undescribably pitiable
misery—yet she was courteous, alert of mind, and
very remarkably aware to the times. During her last
two years, in the midst of that degradation, she
mastered Braille and was reading Drinkwater's play
"Lincoln", shortly before her death.[30]

This description reveals Duncan's great personal sym-
pathy for Fellows, and she was quite explicit in expressing
her sentiments:

a braver, more patient, more kindly-souled person I
have never met. It was these qualities which won
me to the task of piecing together her story—in the
hope that the book would bring her both the
satisfaction life seems to have denied her at every
turn, and a little money to make her last long wait
not so filled with pain and physical discomfort.[31]

Kunigunde Duncan was a Kansas-based, free-lance writer,
mainly for newspapers. Her subject matter varied widely;

[30] Kunigunde Duncan to Mrs. [Margaret Louisa] Riggs, May 20, 1939,
Margaret Louisa Irvine Riggs Collection, in the Archives of the South Dakota
Conference of the United Church of Christ, Center for Western Studies,
Augustana College, Sioux Falls, South Dakota.
[31] Duncan to Riggs, May 20, 1939, Riggs Collection.

she was a music critic for the *St. Louis Star*, a syndicated feature writer for twenty Kansas newspapers, and the author of about three thousand poems, including ones for children, as well as fifteen books. The books included biographies of President Eisenhower's mother and Mentor Graham, one of Abraham Lincoln's teachers, and a novel.[32] She had, however, little knowledge of American Indians or the particular historical setting of Fellows's activities.

A book like this raises two questions about reliability. First, how accurate are the reminiscences of a seventy-six-year-old woman about her life half a century earlier? Second, how much are the views of the collaborator mixed into the final product? Regarding the first question, Duncan acknowledged that "as most grow older they tend to glamorize their youth, their memory fails and they tell of the past, enhaloed."[33] Duncan, however, based her book not only on Fellows's oral reminiscences but also on "a trunkful of letters, government school documents and newspapers."[34] Duncan wrote,

> before I sent out the manuscript to a publisher I took fine pains to check and verify every statement made. Mrs. Tillman had kept all the correspondence of her entire life. In a trunk filled with these letters I was able to verify so much that she said, and usually found that her memory and statement were uncannily true, that the few things I was thus unable to verify I left to the law of averages to take care of.[35]

[32] Barbara Harte and Carolyn Riley, eds., *Contemporary Authors: A Bio-Bibliographical Guide to Current Authors and Their Works* (Detroit: Gale Research Co., 1969), s.v. "Duncan, Kunigunde."

[33] Duncan to Riggs, May 20, 1939, Riggs Collection.

[34] Kunigunde Duncan to Mr. Fox, March 14, 1940, note attached inside cover of the copy of *Blue Star* in the South Dakota State Library, Pierre.

[35] Duncan to Riggs, May 20, 1939, Riggs Collection.

Elaine Goodale Eastman, author of *Sister to the Sioux* and wife of the noted Charles Eastman (Ohiyesa), a mixed-blood Dakota, wrote a book review of *Blue Star* and gave it an endorsement for accuracy: "Since the present reviewer happens to have been familiar with this same aspect of Indian life between 1886 and 1903, it is possible to testify to its essential truth."[36]

In addition, how much did Duncan unknowingly interject herself into the book? A reading of the letters and articles by Corabelle Fellows published in *The Word Carrier* reveals information and attitudes consistent with those expressed in the book. While one cannot verify every detail or phrase, it seems that much of Fellows is represented in *Blue Star*. Duncan, however, introduced confusion by referring several times to the Cheyenne language and culture. At one point Fellows supposedly made "much progress in the Cheyenne tongue" (p. 128), and other passages mention Cheyenne baby lore, a Cheyenne lullaby, an anonymous "Cheyenne youth," and the Teton Sioux language "mixed and mingled" with Cheyenne (p. 143, 145, 159, 160). Even the word list at the end of the book purports to include some Cheyenne words and phrases. Apparently Duncan was misled by the name of the Cheyenne River Indian Reservation. In spite of the name, the people of the reservation were Lakota, not Cheyenne. The Cheyenne River Reservation included persons from the Sans Arcs, Minneconjou, Two Kettles, and Blackfoot bands of Teton Sioux. The Cheyenne were neighbors of the Lakota, and the histories of the two peoples had many similarities, but there is no indication that Fellows had any substantial contact with the Cheyenne. Elaine Goodale Eastman in her review of *Blue Star* stated, "Either she or her collaborator seems to have confused the

---

[36] Elaine Goodale Eastman, "Review of *Blue Star*," *Springfield* (Mass.) *Republican*, Winter 1939, handwritten copy by Margaret Louisa Riggs in Riggs Collection; Elaine Goodale Eastman, *Sister to the Sioux* (Lincoln: University of Nebraska Press, Bison Books, 1978).

Cheyennes,—a distinct tribe with an entirely different language,—with the Cheyenne River Indians among whom she lived."[37] At the end of *Blue Star* Duncan gave credit to Edward Eagle Boy, "a Sioux lad," for assisting her in editing the word list (p. 210). She later identified Eagle Boy as "a fine bright Cheyenne boy."[38] Duncan seems not to have understood the difference and is the likely source of the confusion.

Corabelle Fellows's narrative presents a number of significant themes—about her own motives, about women and children, and about cultural interference and cultural blindness. First, with surprising candor, she revealed that defiance of her parents' wishes was one of the motives behind her decision to work with American Indians. She described her mother as a person preoccupied with having her daughters "marry in a higher walk" (p. 32), "to learn all that was needful to meet and associate with the 'best' people" (p. 38). Fellows plainly stated that choosing to "go west and teach Indians" followed from her determination *not* to "follow the social path which had been so fondly planned for me" (p. 52, 50). She quoted her sister Marian who saw the decision as rebellion, saying to their mother, "She just wants to get away from you and Papa so you can't control her" (p. 55, 56). Even the opposing views of Indians carried the tone of a disputation. With her mother seeing Indians as "loathsome" and "disgusting," in contrast to "cultured" people, never eligible for admission into "the best society" (p. 55-57), Corabelle's contradictory view was to see Indians as "innately fine," who "needed only a little showing how" (p. 53). Among the altruistic protestations of many missionaries and teachers, it is rare to find someone expressly stating a more personal and mundane motive.

Second, Fellows gave much attention to women, children, and family relationships. So many published works

[37] Eastman review.
[38] Duncan to Riggs, May 20, 1939, Riggs Collection.

dealing with Indians and whites or descriptions of Indian cultures rely upon adult male informants—Indian agents, federal military officers, and male Native American leaders—and the interchange focuses on matters of interest to adult males. However much Fellows's reports were filtered through her own cultural perspectives, she contributed by giving attention to women and children that is all too rare. The introductory pages about her own childhood set the tone, and the interest in such matters continued into Fellows's story of life among the Lakota people. Notable examples are the detailed explanations of female domestic tasks, such as gathering beans, sweet potatoes, and wild turnips (p. 101-4), making moccasins (p. 110-11), meat cutting (p. 147-48), or baby care (p. 143-45). The portrayal of Elizabeth Winyan and the information on courting practices and a wedding ceremony and feast also stand out.

Third, Fellows offered many descriptions of Indian life from her perspective, and in this area the reader has to proceed carefully. Her best descriptions were of various everyday activities, such as making pottery or children catching ducks and fish with their hands. When she moved beyond basic reporting and began to interpret social understandings, religious beliefs, or general attitudes, her own cultural biases and assumptions intruded. In such cases we learn more about Corabelle Fellows than about the people she described.

One example relates to the issue of cleanliness. There are many comments, some made in passing, about the need to teach Indians cleanliness (especially p. 167-68). Fellows attempted "to instruct the little boys in the art of the civilized bath" and ostensibly one of the reasons for cutting their hair was "to keep their heads clean." More than matters of hygiene and health were involved. In nineteenth-century white America cleanliness was a cultural value. Some of the expectations were cosmetic and not essential to health, and cleanliness tended to be linked to moral evaluations, as in the adage "cleanliness is next to godliness." An ABCFM missionary in southern Minnesota wrote that the Dakota "seem

enveloped in moral darkness. Their desires are all sensual
& groveling—*all* earthly. Their bodies are filthy & half-clad.
Their minds are in a still worse condition.''[39] Discussions
of physical "filth" ran together with moral and spiritual
degradation in a blurred conjunction of images. In fact,
Fellows admitted that when she traveled for two weeks from
camp to camp with Good Dog and his family, they managed
to keep cleaner than she did (p. 191).

Fellows made frequent comments about the roles of men
and women suggesting that men were lazy and women
burdened in traditional Lakota culture. She advocated "a
more equal division of labor," encouraged men to assist
women in tasks such as carrying wood and water, and
assumed that women should be protected and shielded from
certain aspects of life, especially heavy labor. A newspaper
article written by Fellows from the Cheyenne River Reservation in 1886 clearly revealed her perspectives:

> The sight that grieves me most is to see women
> doing work that is much too hard for them,
> when they have children that need their care
> and strength. It is hard to sit by and see the men
> allow their wives to bring great heavy loads of
> wood upon their backs, while they (the men)
> idle their time away, generally preparing for a
> dance in the evening, with paint, ornaments,
> and feathers. I hope the day will come when
> these heathen customs will be done away with,
> and the man will learn that his first Christian duty
> is to his wife and children; to shield them from
> these things, and be noble enough to do the hard
> work. The women will have to learn to be more
> cleanly, and out of scanty material have their

[39] Joseph W. Hancock to Jabez Brooks, undated letter, Methodist
Episcopal Church, Minnesota Annual Conference Historical Society Papers,
Library and Archives Division, Minnesota Historical Society, St. Paul.

homes pleasant and neat. Oh, how much there is for
most of them to learn.[40]

Lakota religious leaders and practices did not fare well
in Fellows's descriptions. Medicine men were mentioned
only in passing (p. 163-65, 189) and in a tone that implied
that they were both charlatans and rivals. When she described a sweat lodge, she saw it only as an ineffective
medical remedy, totally missing its overarching spiritual
significance as a purification rite.[41] Most striking was her
reaction to the sun dance (p. 117-19). She offered a few
descriptive comments, but even here she misunderstood, as
when she mentioned the "haphazard four-pole shelter which
all these Indians erected hastily for feast or dance." Such
a comment showed no awareness of the careful, elaborate
ritual preparation that preceded the dance. Mostly we learn
of her horror at the sight of blood and the dancing of these
"maddened men" and her flight from the scene in revul-
sion. It is a powerfully descriptive example of a common
non-Indian reaction to the sun dance, but it tells us virtually nothing about the character and meaning of the sun dance
or of its importance to the Lakota. She briefly mentioned
Gray Hawk's comment about suffering but dismissed it; we
learn nothing of the complex symbolism or the understandings of sacrifice and suffering, usually on behalf of others.[42]
If the dance seems too bloody both to Fellows's contem-
poraries and modern readers, dancers might reply that the
symbolism of the rite is little different from that of the Christian religion, which employs the cross, an instrument of tor-
ture and execution, as its central symbol.

[40] Corabelle Fellows, "Among the Wild Indians," *The Word Carrier*,
January 1886, p. 4.
[41] Black Elk, *The Sacred Pipe: Black Elk's Account of the Seven Rites
of the Oglala Sioux,* recorded and edited by Joseph Epes Brown (Norman:
University of Oklahoma Press, 1953), chapter 3; Powers, *Oglala Religion,*
89–91.
[42] Black Elk, *Sacred Pipe,* chapter 5; Powers, *Oglala Religion,* 95–100.

As a teacher, Fellows participated quite fully in the process of Indian acculturation, assuming that replacing the culture of her Indian students with her own was a self-evident good. She showed little awareness of the general context of change in which she was participating, and she did not seem to recognize the trauma of enforced assimilation. Thus she punished children in her own way, even if it violated the tribe's understanding of child rearing and usurped another's authority (p. 186-87). She gave children English first names and used their fathers' names as their last names, ignoring native understandings of naming practices (p. 188). She struggled to change the students' appearance, including their "clinging to blankets" (p. 100) and their hair style (p. 167-68). In many ways she tried to supplant native leadership through her competition with medicine men (p. 114), assumption of parental roles, and challenges to village leadership. On the last point, the story of Old Yellow Hat is especially poignant and tragic (p. 165-67). As the leader of Cut Meat Creek camp he was facing usurpation of his authority by white outsiders. Because it was his responsibility to help educate the young, he made a list of some of the English words Fellows was teaching, borrowed chalk and pencils, and walked off "tall, erect, and dignified," intending to teach the children himself. When children stopped coming to her school, she then threatened to use the power of the federal government (imprisonment) to assert her authority as teacher. He "returned not a word," and the children once again attended the government school. No other story in the book better represents the dynamics of cultural interference, of which Fellows herself was only partially aware.

She also seemed to have an exaggerated view of the honor and importance in which she was held by Dakota and Lakota people. Some of this is a matter of tone. In the cultural encounter each side learned about the other. Yet Fellows discussed what she learned as a matter of course, while describing the children as "marveling" at what she told them

(p. 72) or "enormously delighted" with her clothing and trinkets (p. 126). When she told of being "honored" in a ceremony, however she might have understood the event, there is no indication that the Indians were humbling themselves before her or elevating her above themselves. They thanked her, as an equal, for the attention she was giving to their children (p. 153-54). One may doubt if she was viewed by the children "as a goddess," especially when these same children, showing little deference, took it upon themselves to rename her and preferred articles of her clothing that looked most like the clothing they wore (p. 69-73). They might not mind having a teacher among them, but they would prefer education on their own terms (p. 129).

All of these comments about cultural insensitivity and cultural interference do not gainsay the fact that Corabelle Fellows genuinely cared about the children she worked with, developed significant friendships with native people, and was well intentioned in trying to provide what she thought would be helpful. Her narrative offers a portrait of a teacher among Native Americans, describing her intentions and self-image and reflecting common attitudes of the times. The picture that results is full of ambiguity, with mixed motivations, unintended results, and confusing evaluations. Yet the very complexity of the portrayal makes it valuable, helping us to see a teacher among American Indians not as a stereotyped hero or villain but as a complicated participant in the historical story.

Bruce David Forbes

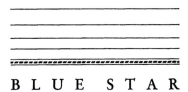

BLUE STAR

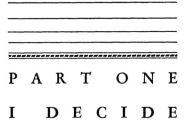

PART ONE

I DECIDE

CHAPTER ONE

I MUST have been very young indeed when my father left home. Humiliated by his having been refused as a soldier in the Civil War, because of a childhood injury to a hip, he had resigned as postmaster and had taken Mother and the children from Princeton, Illinois, to Glens Falls, New York, to remain while he and a Charles Tupper went West to hunt for gold. It was late winter when he returned, and I was three years old.

His return is the first thing I remember: a strange man with very long hair and very queer clothes running into the house, snatching up my mother, and kissing her violently. Then he turned to where my sister Marian and I looked on, somewhat frightened, and tossed us, over and over, into the air, half smothering us with caresses at each catch. Uncle John Haight rushed up to crack him a resounding blow across the back. The two men laughed with loud, excited voices. I wondered why.

For days the family sat, listening wide-eyed to the bizarre tales of what Charlie Tupper and Father had seen and done in strange-sounding places— Colorado, Arizona, Old Mexico. I was too young to be much impressed with what was being said. Later I marveled when I heard the stories retold, for the two men had lived through Indian skirmishes, had frozen, tramped, starved, and at last had found gold. I remember, after that first rush of joy, my father unwound a long pouchy belt from about his waist and laid it on the table. When he opened it, shiny yellow eggs rolled out, and he threw them to us and laughed and shouted with us as Marian and I raced about the room playing with our pretty new toys.

Only one thing is vividly distinct in all the excited talk of that first day. My father took me upon his lap and told me how sorry he was that he hadn't been able to bring on a little red pony with a white saddle that he had bought for us. He told me how he had bought the little beast and led it down to the pier to load it onto the Mexican boat bound for New Orleans, but that the weighmaster had said that it would overload the ship, and he had had to leave the sleek, quiet little thing standing on the pier.

I learned later how Father had been turned back at the Mexican border when he had attempted to return home. He had been obliged to stay many months in Mexico, where he had lived in the sharpest anxiety, for my mother's letters had long since ceased to arrive. She had given up writing after the first year and a half, for no letter my father sent her after he left Colorado ever reached her. She and the family were certain he was dead. At last, in desperation, he had bought a team and wagon and a load of cotton, and hired a man to accompany him as his servant. Arrived at New Orleans with his cargo, he had disembarked, presented the team, wagon, and cotton to his astonished "servant," and had made his own hazardous way up through the South to Glens Falls.

Shortly after Father's return, he reprimanded Marian at table one day for some childish shortcoming in etiquette. She ran from the room, howling. Mother followed to command a return, but Marian held out, saying, "Twange man have no business to 'peak to me 'at way!" But I, I accepted his rebukes gallantly and was friends at once with this nice new man who rode me on his shoulder much oftener and with far more galloping than Uncle John.

Months must have intervened between Father's return and the next incident I recall. I adored Marian. She was even prettier than my doll, I thought, with her long, bobbing curls—my hair was straight—and besides, she had the faculty of being able to say things to people, a power nothing short of miraculous to a little hang-her-head like me. Marian was never at a loss, but could always tell what we should play, or do, or say. I rarely spoke unprompted by her. Imagine my wonder when

one day as I was swinging on the gate a very fine
lady and gentleman passed, and I heard—distinctly
heard the man say to his companion—"What a
pretty little girl!" I ran in excitedly to tell Mother
such an astonishing thing, and added, "He must
have thought I was Marian, Mamma!" How my
mother laughed and laughed, and picked me up
and kissed me on both cheeks, amused at my in-
terpretation of the man's remark.

Just before we left Glens Falls, Mother sent me
to Uncle John's store for soap. I kept the number
of cakes straight and came away with the correct
brand. But outside the door sat a whole row of re-
markable red wagons of assorted sizes. I tried them
all and plunked down my soap in the one that
seemed best to me. I was delighted with the bright,
turning wheels and the unbelievable ease with
which one could transport six cakes of rather heavy
soap. So I did not go directly home, but enjoyed
to the utmost this new and completely satisfactory
method of transportation. At home I drew my
wagon up possessively beside the swing in the yard
and delivered my soap. Next morning the wagon
was gone.

Uncle John was good-natured and loved to toss
Marian into the air. She had a delicious laugh and
shining curls. When he came in one day to dinner
and picked Marian up for the usual frolic, I plucked
timidly at his trouser leg.

"Uncle John," I said, "here's little Corabelle Fellows, too."

He put Marian down and took me instead. I can still hear him say, "This child has been neglected because she is not so handsome. From here on little Corabelle Fellows won't have to remind her Uncle John that she is here too." It was a master stroke as far as I was concerned. Life became a new story, indeed.

It was at Glens Falls, too, that I had my first experience in hating. Our house sat on a beautifully wooded slope overlooking the Hudson River. The cousins came often to play, and our favorite game was telling stories. If I would say tragically, "And the poor little girl's grandmother died dead," one cousin would invariably interrupt with a gush of talk that could not be dammed: " 'N I had a grandmother that dieded, and she ist dieded and dieded. . . . " O how I hated that boy! He always spoiled everything.

Of our trip home from Glens Falls I remember little. Father wished to re-establish himself in his old profession of photography, which he had followed before the war, and we started to return to Princeton, Illinois. But for some reason we went on West and found ourselves in the little town of Glasgow, Missouri. Of all the happenings at Glasgow, one stands out most clearly. I can still see the giant cannon ball rolling in a zigzag course down the slope of a muddy and rutted street.

The ragged end of Price's army was going through, and all the women and children had been sent to the cellars. Our cellar was crowded, and the crowd took turns looking through a chink in the foundation. The soldiers had been in town for days, and had fired roofs, ripped featherbeds, commandeered provisions in stores and pantries, and now, as they were on the point of leaving, they were cannonading the town. Mother said the men had later counted twenty-seven holes in the rooms above our cellar torn by bullets while we were below. I remember how my mother lifted me up to the chink in the stone wall and I peeked out to see the cannon ball rolling slowly at first and then spinning dizzily along in the mud. It did not explode, but rolled on down into the Missouri River.

At Glasgow we boarded. I pitied the old black mammy in the kitchen who, though her baby cried and cried, could not stop what she was doing to tend to it. All the women servants at this place were obliged to leave their little pickaninnies behind and go to the fields. The babies lay about under the trees, but when the sun rose high and the shade would lift, they would howl for mercy there upon the grass in the hot sun.

The noise distracted my mother. She herself would not "touch the little black things," but when I offered to drag them out of the sun she made no objection. So I made it my business to do just that. They interested me tremendously, and I wondered if they wouldn't really make better toys than dolls who, after all, wouldn't cry if you left them in the hot sun. "Those repulsive little niggers," Mother would say. "However can you stand to touch them?" I didn't understand what she could mean. I would run away, wondering, to the kitchen, where I chased the flies away from the cook's baby with the turkey-wing duster and rocked and rocked with engrossed interest until I was rewarded by seeing the little face become composed and the eyelids droop in sleep.

One morning Mother created quite a scene at this boardinghouse. The kitchen mammy had evolved her own idea of an efficient and speedy way of doing things. With her dishpan she went from chair to chair in the dining room and washed each service then and there and restored it to its place. The idea was sound enough, I suppose, but the details of execution were at fault. She forgot to consider that the bottom of the dishpan was blackened with greasy soot. Thus she left a sizable circle of black upon the seat of each dining chair. Dainty as usual, my mother sat down and ate peacefully enough. But when she rose! Her best silk *ruined!* Mammy heard her through in the kitchen without batting an eye or uttering a syllable. Mother spent the morning crying in her room.

Memory freshens now, and events crowd fast. In the little town of Chillicothe, Missouri, Father opened his photograph gallery, and Marian and I were sent to a private school. I remember only that the teacher's name was Miss Lane, but I haven't the dimmest image of how she looked or what she taught. But how different with Marcus Tullius Cicero Williams! Besides being dancing master he had a children's class in Latin. Those Latin forms I mastered then, by the primitive method of saying them over and over, I know to this day. And I see the long tails of "Mr. Alphabet's" coat swing elegantly out behind as he guided his child partners in the waltz, the schottishe, and the gavotte. I see his gleaming mustachios and his polished fingernails. O but he was fine! He taught us, too, to strum the guitar, and I was utterly carried away with the grace of his quirking finger as he played the "Spanish Fandango" with delicate and harmonious strumming.

Chillicothe was the scene of my first lie and of two of the four spankings I ever received—and these within half an hour of each other. Mother was baking pumpkin pies and needed additional milk. Little as I was, I was sent for it. I set out with the bright tin pail and had returned part of the way, when I stumbled and spilled the milk. Frankly, I recount, no Washingtonian ghost of ancestral integrity arose to allay either my terror or my rapid mental calculations. I ran back to the house and asked for more milk.

"All right," the woman said, as she poured it through her strainer of cloth into my pail, "but I can't spare as much as you got before." A small matter to a four-year-old, surely.

Proud and completely conscience-free, I delivered the milk into my mother's none too patient hand. She had waited overlong in the midst of pie baking.

"Why, she hasn't sent what I asked for," said Mother, even before she set down the pail.

"She said she couldn't spare it," I countered.

My father was in the kitchen. He now looked sternly at me. "This child is not telling the truth," he said. "Corabelle, come with me."

Back we went over my tragic trail, came upon the little pool of milk collected in the depression where I had tripped, went to the woman's house.

"Mrs. Fellows sent for a quart," Father said courteously. "She is baking pumpkin pies and needs a full quart."

"I gave Corabelle a quart the first time," said this woman who could speak only truth, "but the second time I couldn't spare it."

"Thank you," said my father.

Arrived home, my whole wretched drama was re-enacted through the report Father made to Mother. Having reached the climax, he took me

firmly across his knee and gave me a few gentle
spanks. I might have recovered my equanimity
shortly, for I was much more surprised than injured, had Father not sealed my doom by thrusting
me into the depths of a clothes closet. "Corabelle
Fellows," he said sternly as he shut the door, "never,
never lie again."

With a sudden rush of anger and revenge I felt
up in the dark. On tiptoe I managed to reach,
yank and tug from their hooks and hangers
all the best clothes of the family and let them fall
about me as they would. When my fifteen-minute
incarceration was ended and Mother came to re-
lease the prisoner, she found a tearless and defiant
face turned up to hers. Her spanking was without
restraint, and left me humiliated and very thought-
ful concerning the goodness of parents, a thing
which, before, I had had no reason to doubt.

Encouraged by my mother, who loved cities, my
father soon disposed of the Chillicothe business and
we removed to Chouteau Avenue in St. Louis,
where he opened quite a pretentious studio. The
look of the reflecting skylight, the strange odor that
came out of his little coal-black developing den, the
fine ladies who came to pose, the brilliantly painted
screen upon which floated a life-sized swan—all
these things had a great fascination for me. Never
shall I forget the German matron who came, bringing her little boy and a great dog to pose. The

little boy, after having been screwed into one un-
comfortable position after another by my father
—directed by his mother—began suddenly to howl.
They took him up on the roof. Here he bellowed.
I trailed up after them to watch. At last the mother
applauded what she wanted: the boy leaning lov-
ingly against the dog after the manner of a colored
picture card she had brought along as guide. Father
had spoiled twenty plates. When she came for the
proofs she said, "Noon of deze vaver my Hermann,
mine Herr," and swept out grandly. For a long
time we kept one picture Father finished, a picture
of a tousle-headed boy, his mouth distended in the
utmost travail of angry weeping, while one hand
rested woodenly on the haunch of the obliging,
mellow-eyed dog.

There was a second skylight in the hall of our
apartment, for we lived in the same building with
the studio. There wasn't any place for a child to play
except in this hall or upon the paved court below.
As Christmas approached, Marian and I became
really worried. Upon examination we located a
chimney higher up than our windows on the building, but there was none, not a trace of one, on our
floor. Could Santa Claus get through a skylight?
We craned our necks and tried to imagine just how
a fat man could do it, but we viewed the situation
with growing alarm. Finally we put the decision
up to Father. "Why, certainly," said Father. "Sure.

Of course." Thus assured, we waited in rapt expectancy.

We had asked for but one thing, a doll's cradle. Santa brought it—a most astonishing replica of the one in which a new baby brother, Clement, lay on Christmas morning, fast asleep. Two dolls lay beneath a silk quilt, a miniature of the one on Mother's bed. Beside the cradle lay two little boxes deftly covered in shirred pink and blue silk in the most divine tints. And we had only asked for a cradle! And the boxes! They held tiny scissors, thimbles, flowered and silken rolls of fabrics that looked like fairy things. "Mothers with children have to make clothes for them," said our mother.

Speechless with joy, we turned back the silk quilt of the cradle. Two rag-bodied china-headed dolls lay there. They had no clothes on at all! We could make them! That there were play dishes, too, was unbelievable, for our only toy had been one rag doll for the two of us. So we learned to sew, and, little as we were, Mother read aloud to us as we stitched—all of Louisa Alcott's books and some of Dickens'.

We were living in St. Louis on Chouteau Avenue when Lincoln was shot, April 4, 1865. I remember vaguely how Mother took us out with her to a neighbor's, where everybody talked more softly than usual and looked solemn, and nobody laughed at all. Mother told us that the President of the

United States had been killed, and that everybody
was sorry because he had been such a great and
good man. I tried to be sorry, too. It seemed
proper to be. But I didn't succeed. To hide my
ignominious cheerfulness I got behind our settee
and played with my doll clothes and wished I had
a kitten to dress up like the little girl had where
Mother had taken us to talk about our "noble
President" who had been killed by an awful bad
man.

And not long after this Mother gave us the
cat—not a kitten, but a great sober old Tom for
which, with my own eyes, I saw her put three
shining dollars into the dirty palm of the same
little boy who ran whooping down our street every
day, in a way we were not permitted to whoop, and
who stopped every now and then to give someone
a paper from the pile under his arm. The cat was
dirtier than the boy. Marian and I giggled at his
droll, smudged face as he sat blinking solemnly.
All the time Mother was bathing him we hopped
up and down in delighted anticipation. He must
have appreciated the bath, for he submitted to it
with dignity, without a yowl or a scratch and,
afterwards, sat obediently in a towel to dry. I can
see him yet, so serious and dripping, aiding his
toilet with tongue and paw to the amazed delight
of Marian and me who watched intently but
couldn't find out how he did it.

Many, many happy hours we spent dressing old Tom in clothes which were our idea of what "fine ladies" wore. He always appeared mildly scornful, sitting or walking about with undisturbed gravity, though we would be howling with laughter at a twitch of the ear that had tilted his lady's sailor at a rakish angle over one eye. When I was seventeen and teaching little children, I recalled the hours with old Tom and wrote this little verse to please those children:

There was a playhouse long ago
Beneath the rafters rude and low
Where herbs and seed-corn hung to dry,
The property of Madge and I.
Now let's play this and let's play that:
I'll be the man and wear the hat,
You be the woman with long curls,
And dollies be our little girls.
And fat old Tommy with pink nose
Let's dress up in the baby's clothes.

Even yet I remember those days with pleasure. Living was a happy thing indeed.

While my lie was my chief Chillicothe memory, my running away to the circus is my chief memory connected with St. Louis. Mother was ill, and Father had taken Marian and me to the studio with him so that we should not disturb her. It was a busy day for him, for the circus was in town, and country people were swarming into the studio to have their pictures made. Father gave us two

chairs by the windows and told us to sit there until
we had his permission to move. Marvel of mar-
vels! Right down below me was the biggest tent
in the world! Crowds of people waving flags,
music of a band, and a general commotion should
have been entertainment enough for anybody. So
it was—for awhile.

"What is a circus, Papa?" I asked him on one of
his infrequent trips through the outer room of the
studio.

His answer was dumfounding: "Animals from
all parts of the earth, acrobats"—whatever could
acrobats be?—"feats of all kinds——"

I looked at my feet—*of all kinds?* I slipped down
from my chair, unheeding Marian's warning,
"Papa said not to," and making my way upstairs, I
stole into our apartment, got my little drab ulster
and hat, ran down three flights of stairs, out across
the congested thoroughfare, and, trotting breathlessly, gained the big tent. Fighting through an
army of legs, I gained the miraculous interior. A
very nice man in a red coat picked me up. I disclosed readily enough that I was on a self-directed
tour, without guide. He carried me from cage to
cage and I clung desperately to him at times when
big eyes and mouths and trunks came perilously
near. We were having the very nicest of times
when we met my father, hatless and perspiring. I
was ruthlessly taken from the arms of my enter-

tainer and carried back ignominiously to the studio, where I was deposited amid a fearful and forecasting silence upon the chair from which I had so lately slipped.

Father said absolutely nothing to me all afternoon, but I got my third spanking as soon as we went upstairs that night, and it was not a few gentle spats. Besides, I had to sit on a chair another whole hour. This wasn't so bad, for I had Mother's hourglass to watch, and I was quite contented to watch the fine white sand sifting gently down. The awful suspense of not knowing what Father would do to me, which I had suffered all afternoon, was gone. I enjoyed myself by recalling the elephants and giraffes and hippopotamuses and lions. Marian didn't even know the names of them, and no nice man in a red coat had carried her and told her!

CHAPTER TWO

FATHER was of New Hampshire stock and loved the country. He was a surveyor by choice, but had learned photography for my mother's sake so that she might live in her beloved city. He told us many tales of his own father, who, with his dog, Growler, had roamed the New Hampshire hills to his heart's content when he was a little boy. He had caught porcupines! Father had roamed those same hills, too, and Father once caught two porcupines the same day. His eyes glowed as he recounted his escapades. He always dwelt upon the beauty of the country: the trees, the snuggling homestead, and the river. Marian and I made a smock for old Tom, such a garment as answered Father's description of the smock his father wore when he was a little boy. But we never could get Tom to walk back and forth and run our spool-box butter churn, according to Grandfather's recipe in which he had used old Growler.

Mother enlivened us with enthusiastic descriptions of her party dresses she had had as a child and later when she had attended the seminary at Glens

Falls. She had been educated in music, French, needlework, and fine cookery. Father must have won in their private discussions, for we left St. Louis to live on a farm near Richmond, Missouri. I whooped like a savage to be freed from the prison of the Chouteau apartment with its paved court.

I thought Father's flock of sheep of perhaps a hundred the most wonderful in the world. Marian and Clement and I had one pet lamb after another, for the weakling lambs or one of a pair of twins were brought to the house for Mother's care. Only when a lamb became strong enough to butt us over were we willing to relinquish it for another weak baby that could be cuddled. We had a burro, too, who objected to carrying double and got his way in the matter by the simple expedient of trotting along under the low growth at the edge of the wood until he had dislodged one passenger.

We little girls were not permitted to go to the stock pens, but once Father took me with him when they were driving white Chesterfield hogs to the Richmond market. There were several teams and wagons. I rode with Father upon what seemed to me the dangerously high seat of the new wagon. Most of the drove walked all of the way, but, as the fattest ones tired and held back the others, they were lifted, squealing horribly, into the wagons. Though most of them walked the ten miles, the wagons were all filled by the time we reached Richmond. I was safe with Father on the high seat and got a fine chill of delight in watching the grunting, heaving, squealing animals that could not get up where I was.

The farm home at Richmond is clear in my mind: a large rambling two-story house set among locusts and elms. A veranda ran around three sides, and on the fourth stood the two-bucket well. Mother always had petunias, phlox, four-o'clocks, and cosmos in the summer. In the winter we lived mostly in the kitchen and the great living room on the first floor. Both rooms had fireplaces. In the very coldest weather Mother cooked in the iron pot that hung from a crane in the living room fireplace. Father rolled in the fragrant backlog across the blue-and-red-striped rag carpet. The brass andirons, the crane with its pot, the fire screen, and the strong black tongs and shovel were hearth companions of us children, who lay reading in the light and warmth.

There was no school available. Mother became our teacher, and was most exacting and demanding. She furnished an upstairs room with desks, books, and writing materials. Here Marian and I studied alone until we were able to repeat without error the lessons she assigned, not five, but six days of the week. We studied writing, reading, arithmetic, geography, physiology, and sewing. No lesson could be recited immediately after any little girl reported, "Mother, I know it now." No, indeed. Lessons must be let "get cold." Anybody can sit down and memorize a lesson and say it right away—and then forget it. Mother said if you really learned it you would be able to say it if someone woke you up at midnight and asked you to say it. Always when we least expected it, Mother would call us to her and demand the spelling of words, the boundaries of a state, the multiplication table, or the poem she had set us to learn, or ask us to write a paragraph on the circulation of the blood. Two books rise up before me, clean and un-dogeared, for Mother permitted no untidiness— Sanders' second reader and the blue-black speller.

We sewed an hour every day. Of course we had our catechism to learn for Sunday. Mother was determined that even if we were just a farmer's daughters our education should not suffer. We might marry in a higher walk. Not that Father was uneducated or uncaring. He spent much time with his philosophers and poets, but the urge of outdoor life was just stronger than the pull of culture.

I wonder if Mother wasn't right to be so exacting of us, for, as I sit blind in my old age, the verses of poetry, the answers to questions I learned there in that upstairs room, pass through my mind and are supremely comforting.

Marian was demure and conventional. I was eternally doing what wasn't the thing to do. Marian accepted. I inquired as long as no one checked my path. Take church. *Why* shouldn't you turn your head and look around? *What* was back there? One Sunday as I sat, face front, beside Marian, I resolved to find out *right then* what was in the *back* of a church. With a sudden dash, boldly, in the face of all Marian's whispered commands, pleadings, threats, and leg-pullings, I squirmed to my knees and looked over the pew back. I saw a woman, a very small woman, but for all her littleness, frightfully alarming. One entire side of her face was covered with a brilliant purple-red splotch. I was terrorized but spellbound. I couldn't look away! I gazed intently at the glowing color, which seemed to be growing more vivid, until the woman's eyes drew mine. They bulged out very far and glistened fearfully, reminding me of dragons in stories. I completed my scandalous behavior by banging violently against Marian as I righted my position, knocking her hat as much askew as my own. It was a long time before I tried again to learn more of the rear of church interiors.

After we had become habituated to studying, Mother began to demand general reading in addition to the school program. Both Marian and I became "bookies," and it must have gratified Mother immensely to see us reading hour upon hour. After lessons, sewing, reading, catechism, we could play! The question and answer method of instruction that Mother used may have been poor pedagogy, but it was a deadly certain way of making essential information adhere.

One day Mother told us that our cousin, Ida Fobes, was coming to see us. Goodness gracious! She was that mythical Cousin Ida who sent such unimaginably lovely dolls and frocks from Washington, D. C., capital of the United States of America! (Question 2, page 30.) Mother added to our apprehension by saying that she was very elegant indeed and that we would certainly have to watch our P's and Q's every minute she was visiting, so as not to disgrace the family. We studied our etiquette books assiduously. Our anticipation was a mixture of engulfing troughs of feeling perfectly inadequate to the ordeal, and exhilarating crests following our private etiquette rehearsals. When the day actually arrived we were somewhat cocky, and waited excitedly in the hall for the arrival of Cousin Ida Fobes, from Washington, D. C., capital of the United States of America. We always said it all.

Most elegant she proved to be. She was pretty, dressy, talented, and made our house ring with her laughter and singing and piano playing. But these were the least things. She could write! Marian and I were in complete awe of her. Here was one of

Corabelle Fellows at eight

Corabelle's Brother Clement

that kind of people who put down words in books for children to learn and *remember all their lives!*

Clement was a Little Lord Fauntleroy lad by now, with brown curls to his shoulders, as was the mode of the times, and with great brown eyes. Mother had had him at memorizing, too, and he delighted Cousin Ida with his ability to recite several lengthy poems. Mother was quilting one day, and Clement walked round and round the frames, rehearsing his store of Shakespeare. Ida caught him up and took him off with her. When they came in to supper, Clement had added excerpts from *Antony and Cleopatra* to his repertoire.

He and Cousin Ida adored each other and went everywhere together. When she began to talk of returning to Washington she begged Mother to let her take Clement with her for a short stay. Then she began talking earnestly to both Father and Mother about how they were "wasting themselves on a farm and depriving their children of proper privileges." Actually, before she left, Cousin Ida had persuaded Father to remove to Washington. Mother, of course, was more than eager to go. It was decided that Ida should take Clement with her and save Mother so much in the turmoil of moving.

Her first letter back was sparkling. She and Uncle Edson, her father, had visited the Congress with Clement. At recess, in the Senate chamber, they had stood Clement in the Speaker's place

where, to the astonishment of the senators still at
their desks, he had stood unafraid, and in a dashing
fashion had given the whole of "Jim Bledsoe," a
long narrative poem by John Hay, once American
ambassador to England, who was also the author of
"Little Britches." Clement had gone through with
the heroics of Jim Bledsoe who, captaining one of
two racing boats, ran his ship aground when he
saw that she was ablaze, and held her fast to the
shore until all the passengers were safely landed,
losing his own life by the act. The opening lines
as little Clement used to speak them are clearly
with me:

> Whar hev y' bin these last three year
> That y' havn't heerd folks tell
> How Jimmy Bledsoe passed in his checks
> The night of the Prairie Belle?

The next letter sent Mother in haste to Washington. Clement had scarlet fever. He died before
Mother reached him. When Cousin Ida and Uncle
Edson met Mother at the station they told her
only, "He is with us yet."

They had laid the little fellow upon a white
pillow on the red plush divan, his curls careless, his
posture that of sleep. At sight of him Mother
smiled and went softly over, but when she realized
the awful truth she fell senseless, and it was
several days after the funeral that she regained
consciousness.

Thus our removal to Washington was bleakness itself. My parents had lost their first child, a son, before Marian and I were born. Father never recovered from the loss of Clement. He delved among his poets and philosophers while Mother bravely tried to recover her old buoyancy and zest in life. Too, we had come "on the spur of the moment," without suitable precaution. There appeared to be no opening for a photographer or a surveyor. Father got some brief employment with a photographer and finally went to work as doorkeeper at the Capitol. His was the second of the three doors.

We had taken a four-floor house with dormers on the fourth floor. The rear windows commanded a view of Capitol Hill. From the front we could see over most of the city. Father went to work daily but was not happy. Mother worked desperately hard but had much unwanted leisure, since Marian and I were both in the public school and little Clement was dead.

Our grief was somewhat softened by visits of Mother's congressman relatives. Thomas Updegraff, and Rachel and Bess, his daughters, and his wife came often. They were homesick for their Iowa home. Cousin Hatcher came too, with his daughter, Floy. He was a representative from Missouri. By degrees Mother began going out with them, at first to small, and then to larger functions.

By degrees she regained something of her old spirit
and ambition. There were progressive euchre parties at our house for the card players and musicales
for the music lovers. She talked much to Marian
and me about the necessity of social training, and
saw to it that we lost no opportunity to learn all
that was needful to meet and associate with the
"best" people.

What queer fragments lodge in one's mind! Marian and I at first played often on the Capitol steps
to be near Father, for we were companionless and
at a loss to know what to do. Mother dressed us in
the prettiest of clothes. For Sunday, merino, and
for weekdays, colored cambric. Low-neck, short
sleeves held by clasps of pearl or coral, short waists,
full skirts, pantalettes peeping beneath, white
stockings, and black slippers with buckles—these
we wore with pride, for Mother was a fine seam-
stress and had good taste as well. Always we wore
three stiff linen petticoats, and our hair was confined in a net.

I had many magnificently vague ideas about
government as I played, a child, there on the marble
steps of the Capitol. After all these years, the one
clearest memory is that my Father said the inner
stairs were made of "Tennessee marble." I never
hear the word "Capitol" but what I hear my
father say, "Corabelle, these steps are of Tennessee
marble." It had a magnificent sound to me, and I

was convinced that what went on within must be as flawless as those words sounded.

Marian and I liked school: it was so much easier than Mother. We liked the other children and soon became happy and satisfied. During those school years our lives were uneventful, Father going to work every morning and Mother being more and more taken by parties.

When we had first arrived Father had taken us to see Washington Monument, then in process of construction. Great stones lay all about, helter-skelter. Father said the countries of the world had given them. For some reason the work was interrupted, and the stones lay about for years while the already finished part of the monument grew yellow with backwater.

We became familiar with the great Library and other public buildings. I spent much time in the Corcoran Art Gallery and can see in memory the "Greek Slave" and the "Venus de Milo." I went with Father into the dome of the Capitol where he told me how an Italian painter who had designed and painted the mural of the dome had fallen to his death when he was at work on the last section. It was years before anyone could be got to complete the mural. We took dancing and piano lessons, Marian and I. But the richest memory is of reading the books obtained at the Congressional Library. Uncle Updegraff obtained issues of books and we carried them home by the armload. We became the bookiest of booky families, each of us with his nose in a book almost constantly. I read everything I could lay hands on.

We went often to listen to speeches in the Congress. We attended public receptions for the Presidents. Mother began to take Marian and me with her to teas and musicales. Then one night Father came home with the upsetting news that he had leased a farm in Virginia!

Mother consented to go—at last, but most unwillingly. As for me, I grew daily more like father. I rejoiced at the prospect of the freedom of farm life. Marian and Mother wept.

How can I forget my father's voice, apologetic, yet ringing with a joy that could not be concealed, as he pridefully recounted to Mother the riches to which she was going: a thousand fruit trees—apricot, plum, cherry, apple, peach, pear, quince, seven kinds of grapes—I can remember but five: Isabella, Concord, Catalpa, Mitchell, Delaware—strawberries, blackberries, celery, artichokes. Old Uncle Peter, who had always worked this land, would be there, and good old black Kate, his wife, and Bayless, and Jake the German hand, and she might have a table girl, too, if she liked.

The farm proved to be all that Father promised, and more. A great old sixteen-room house sat in the midst of beeches, chestnuts, and oaks, stately

Corabelle Fellows and Her Sister Marian Entertaining a Friend at "Tea"

Toilet Table of Martha Washington, Photographed by
Homer Fellows

and grand enough to make even Mother draw her breath in suddenly. A lawn swept down to the rear of the premises to the cattle and chicken runs. Within, the halls were wide, the rooms larger than any we had ever occupied. There was a veranda around the first floor and a portico on the second.

To me it was paradise. Mother, too, soon acquired the idea that it was possible to be a lady even in the country. We eased, almost at once, into cheerful, peaceful living. We had occasional outings on the Potomac River, for which we helped Mother make much-beruffled organdies and dimities. There were dances on the moonlit decks of steamboats to the music of the piano. There were golden hours spent with friends from Washington, for Mother's prowess as a cook and entertainer kept us in frequent guests.

There was the meticulous canning to be done. The cellar was filled with hundreds of jars of jams and jellies and preserves. Father always had the cider and wine casks full. He was most particular about his grapes. Each bunch had to be carefully cut with scissors and laid gently on a bed of grape leaves. We sometimes helped with this, Marian and I.

Besides the sale of fruit, Father was growing rich fast from the sale of yellow Cochin chickens and from boarding city horses. We, the young ladies, never went down to the stock runs and barns. We kept our own rooms tidy and our clothing made and mended, helped with the cooking, studied, and practiced on the piano. Of course there was the school problem again. Mother set us to reading Russian, French, Spanish, and English history. We made weekly trips into Washington where Uncle Edson taught us astronomy and philosophy and where we had dancing and piano lessons.

We had little time to ourselves, for our clothing was a great time taker, what with ruffles and flounces and hand hemming on petticoats. Mother taught me to darn, and I became so expert that she turned the family darning over to me. I took the keenest pride in my smooth, even work. It could scarcely be told from the fabric. I especially loved to mend linen.

All this in summer. As schooltime approached, Mother decided we should attend the near-by Georgetown Academy. At first we made the trip daily, but the highway was so infested with marauding gangs of blacks and whites that Mother rented a room in Georgetown and we went home over week ends. Every Monday morning we were driven in laden with more roast chicken, jam, fresh-baked bread, jelly, and cake than two girls were likely to eat in twice a week. We took apples and raw potatoes, too, to bake before the grate.

Reared as we had been on meaty reading, and grimly warned against pernicious novels, Marian

and I obediently took up our studies at Georgetown Academy, and all went well—for awhile.
Across from the school stood a quaint and, to me,
mysteriously enticing white house with trim green
shutters. It had two wings that seemed to have
been added after the main part had been built.
There was the usual white picket fence and gravel
path and fan-lighted doorway overhung with the
deep green of a vine. The black knocker on the
door, a long thin one, stood out sharply against the
white panelling of the door. The girls said a
writer lived there!

For a long time I was content just to look at it
and try to imagine what its inhabitant might be
like, for the girls said she lived alone. I always
stopped a second to look out of the windows that
gave a view of this house. It fascinated me. Then
came an inspiration. I was old enough. I knew
how to deport myself. I would call! I would not
wait another day! When the recess bell sounded I
walked directly across the street—against rules—
pushed open the white picket gate and started up
the path. The gate banged harshly, because, as I
discovered when I turned guiltily around, it was
weighted by a rusty flatiron attached to a rusty
chain. Relieved, I went on up to the door and let
the knocker fall. A white-haired woman opened
the door. I introduced myself according to the
well-learned formula, and she asked me to enter.

Her eyes twinkled, but her face was grave. We fell easily into talk. Her desk was piled with papers; she had evidently been writing. I asked her if she had.

"Yes. I write stories. Do you like stories? How about reading one of mine, and you tell me if it is quite right?"

"I shall be delighted and complimented as well," I answered in my best form.

She lifted a few sheets from the pile beside her, and I listened to a chapter from—Heavens! *This was a novel,* the very thing in which my mother knew perdition dwelt! Had I but known how right my mother was! I looked at the gentle, white-haired lady reading in a low voice things that burned me with their newness and intensity. Mother and her novel warning vanished completely. Could I get more like this to read?

She named a few. She lent me the last one published. On wings of a mighty and new emotion I ran out unceremoniously, the book under my arm, and regained my seat—in time and unreprimanded.

Next grade time Mother faced Marian and me sternly. Why the fall in standings? Not *much* of a fall, we countered. But, still a *fall,* Mother decreed. Blanching, I spoke up, hastening to say that we had been reading novels, but that, truly, we had read our last, that it should never occur again—purposely using Father's phrase. When

Father said, "Never let this occur again," the thing was as good as accomplished. Mother contained her anger and made only a few cutting comments when she saw our evident contrition. We returned to Georgetown next Monday, chastened and virtuous in resolution.

And we did prepare our lessons, *first,* thereby somewhat annulling the twinge of conscience. But we succumbed to the novel fever to what we realized was a wholly damning extent. We rarely retired before one, a thing that, in itself, was an unpardonable atrocity. The potatoes and apples always burned, and our standings never returned to their pristine heights. For I returned again and again to the house across the street and got more names of novels and listened to more entrancing chapters. I memorized whole pages of Byron and became as silly and sentimental a girl at sixteen as could be found anywhere. Our room, on the third floor of the Hunter house, had dormer windows. In one of these windows I lolled away many an hour, looking dreamily out over the roofs of the town to the beautiful Potomac River, like the languid ladies in the books, and feeling perfectly qualified in the miraculous subject of love to feel with the best of them.

Often the white gate swung to with a clang of its rusted flatiron, and I spent unreal hours in the dim study with the linnet singing, or merely considering the talk with a round and unfeeling eye. Not until the winter was nearly over and my friend, the writer, and I had become intimate, did I dare to tell her just where and how her story was unsatisfying. I never noticed title pages for eagerness to get at the reading. One day by chance I read a volume, Emma, Dorothy, Eliza, Nezette Southworth—she was E.D.E.N. Southworth! The pages she first lent me to read were from *Gloria*. This book she was at work on at our first meeting was *The Lost Heir of Linlithgow*. I read copiously of Mrs. Southworth's books, but now I can recall but few titles.

One poem I memorized to buoy up my homemade phantasies, opened thus:

"Lone, lone, alone, all, all alone. . . . "

This I quoted aloud in Marian's absence, meanwhile imagining myself to be the forlorn maiden whose lover had been ruthlessly torn away by harsh and unfeeling parent—or guardian. How it came that I read *Don Quixote*, I don't know, unless it was that Mother's novel-reading warnings had been directed particularly against Ouida, and *Don Quixote* sounded foreign and therefore likely to be flavorful. I was profoundly disappointed. *Thaddeus of Warsaw* I read, too, merely because the title sounded romantic. But *Lena Rivers* I devoured.

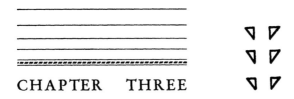

CHAPTER THREE

For TWO years we attended the academy at Georgetown, and I spent the most idyllic months in the summers that my life has ever known. I can never forget the peace, the beauty, the security, there under the spreading beeches and chestnuts. We went out to an occasional festive party in new and dainty dresses, and there were river-boat excursions several times during the summer, but for the most part our life was a peaceful round of practicing music, reading—history, again—and sewing under the trees, a round that looms as most unreal and pastoral above the events of rude and harsh living which later have been mine.

Mother won again. We went back to Washington, this time to Maryland Avenue. Father set up a photograph studio, and I learned to do retouching, which is going over each picture with the utmost nicety, altering facial lines or mending faults in the paper with a fine pen and India ink. We went oftener to Uncle Edson for astronomy and philosophy and attended dancing class regularly. Two piano lessons a week, not one, and a great supply of clothes, which Mother now insisted upon, called for the funds which did not flow from the photograph gallery as they had from the orchard and stock pens of the Virginia farm. Mother let out the top—the fourth—floor to a more dashing, handsomer, altogether more heavenly young man than had ever figured in my dormer dreams at Georgetown.

He was British. He was blond. He was captain of the British Royal Guards—though it never occurred to me to question why he was working in America in the Treasury Building, if this last statement were true. And—he was divinely tall. He was also more than thirty-five.

I had been somewhat interested in two Spanish gentlemen who had first had the rooms, a Mr. Meline and a Mr. Verastique, but it was their smile-provoking English, not their personalities, that interested me. Now this big, bragging Englisher laughed at *my* pronunciation. It infuriated Mother, but I, at seventeen, was taken by storm and obediently imitated his "pairfact" language. Now, at seventy-six, I can see that it was his foreign-looking tweeds and the odor of his brown Windsor soap—experienced so soon after my novel-reading orgy—that were the amazingly large factors in my enthrallment.

Now my knowledge of verse suited to tragic love stood me in stead. My father, without ceremony, turned the man out and ordered him to stay away. "Lone, lone, alone...." I quoted it hourly, shut myself up in my room as the books suggested, refused to eat.

But a letter came, and a temporary paradise was restored. Mrs. Southworth was right. Things did happen according to her ideas. The letter appointed a rendezvous. If there were any danger of his being seen, he would bring a letter and lay it beneath the rock just as you turned off the bridge in the park. And would I bring my missive, too—in case it was impossible for him to appear personally —and place it beneath the same rock? To the relief of the household I came downstairs dressed for the street. I was going, I told them, to see a friend. With the elevated spirit of a saint—a conscienceless saint—I kept my tryst. Evidently danger threatened, for he did not appear. I lifted the rock, took the letter lying beneath it, kissed my own vowful one, laid it carefully down, restored the rock, and rose to return home. There stood—my father! How, after that quart of spilled milk at Chillicothe, could I have thought to doubt his lie-detecting sense?

"Destroy that," he ordered.

I fumbled the letter in my fingers, my first love letter. I had not seen a word of it.

"Do you hear?"

In a tempest of tears and sobs I tore my unread

note into tiny bits and sent them scattering on
the wind.

"Get that letter you put under the stone."

Trembling almost too much to take a step, I did
his bidding. He took my letter from my unresist-
ing hand, took my arm, turned me about. All the
way home, with the greatest sternness I had ever
heard in his voice, and with absolute finality, he
declaimed steadily upon my lover's advanced age,
upon his questionable motives, upon my innocence
and youth. Though I was humiliated and grieved
beyond endurance, I got a kind of bleeding joy out
of it, for was I not suffering even as those heroines
of print for whom I had shed many, many scalding
tears?

As he talked I returned not a word. But there,
coming up Maryland Avenue, my father's sustain-
ing and not ungentle arm in mine, I made my decision. Never, never, would I follow this social
path which had been so fondly planned for me and
for which I was being groomed.

Even before this dramatic, breast-heaving walk
with my father, I had only endured the "functions"
to which I "must go." I thought these Washington
society women a set of silly ninnies to spend their
lives in a round of pretty parties. Always my weak
objections to going had been so completely talked
down by Marian and Mother, that up to this time
I had been docile and given in and gone. Now, as

I walked along, I made a holy vow before God. From now on I should utterly refuse to have a thing to do with this frippery.

Before this Britisher had come to our house I had not only helped Father in his studio, but I had also taken up painting and had progressed through pencil, pen, charcoal, and water color to oils. I had, too, done a little "slumming." I had taught a private school in the unused chapel of an old church. Here I had hung my canary at the window, helped to tack down the bright new carpet and hang the frilled curtains Father had financed for me, and personally solicited pupils. I had twenty-eight.

Now that my heart was broken and love fled forever, I gave myself savagely to teaching and painting. For awhile I kept on at the dancing academy —for even a maiden with a lost lover may hearken to pretty compliments from such a dapper and altogether agreeable dancing master as Professor Marino. Though I loved the rhythms of the dance and the music and the pretty talk, after a short time I stopped attending the dancing school.

I was diminutive, slender, pale, red-eyed. I carefully examined my image in my mirror—according to the romantic recipe—and met a very weak and wilted-looking person, indeed. What I thought was, "If my hair was only curly!" but what I said aloud was, "They'll be surprised!" I remembered from the books that a degree of high drama was

always the appropriate comeback. "Surprise" was
a poor word. "They" were practically paralyzed
by what I did next.

When I spoke those momentous words, I really
had no idea just what to do. But Uncle Updegraff
took me to a meeting of some kind where Senator
John Logan was in attendance. Here I found my
reprieve. Mr. Logan sat tossing his black hair, telling of Indians. I would go West and teach Indians!

My foiled and harassed parents didn't know
which way to turn. At last they decided to order
me to Aurora, Illinois, where I was to stay with
Aunt Ticy Shaw and attend the seminary. They
sent Marian to Aunt May Hewett's in Michigan.
Thus was I "disciplined." Mother outlined my
course: dancing, German or French, and piano. I
went, and for two years stayed and studied obediently. I had a hard time studying at Aunt Ticy's,
for her five children were noisy and disturbing. I
obtained a job as maid for an Eleanor Eggleston,
a school acquaintance. She stood as final proof of
Mrs. Southworth's verity. She was a ward. Her
guardian was a rich man who intended to marry
her. I cooked for the two of them to earn my
board and room. They attended the Baptist
Church. I had been first an Episcopalian, then a
Presbyterian.

Whereas two summers back I had been madly in
love and had scorned all other spheres for a woman,

now I madly scorned love. I greedily absorbed every word of the sermons on the missionary. The red man, as I had met him on the history page, seemed innately fine. He needed only a little showing how. Henceforth my life was to be spent for the Indian.

Without finishing the second year I boarded the eastbound train. Arriving thus unexpectedly, I came in and announced my determination before removing my wraps. Had I been a whole regiment of tall, blond, and handsome British Royal Guards I could scarcely have been a source of greater alarm. Father, Mother, and Marian were all convinced that I was mildly insane. They tried talking gently to me; they tried pleading; they begged. I was iron. I could have gone against my parents' wish. I had considered it. But in those days such an act would have been an unpardonable sin. So I just held out, and held out, during March, April and May, June and July, August and September.

Then I thought I detected a slight weakening in Father. He called me to him and reopened the discussion. He looked at me kindly, and I thought his eyes twinkled ever so little. His eyes were blue like mine, and his hair was straight.

"Corabelle," he said, "about this notion of yours —don't you realize, child, what a slight little body you have? Indians are big, burly people. Their country out there in Dakota is rough and uncivilized. Besides, it is very cold—and you know you have a cough."

"Yes, Papa, I know I have," I said briskly, "but you know a change of climate is always recommended for coughs. Besides, I am only going to teach, and not plow, and you know yourself that my tongue is not weak."

"Why, Corabelle, your experience of the world is scarcely nothing!" He had tackled another point!

"That is probably true," I answered. A sentence out of some book rose up in my mind. "I have some knowledge. You and Mamma have seen to that, and knowledge is but the condensed experience of the race."

"And what idea have you about what it is to work?"—another point won!

I confessed my term as maid. I could cook as well as sew. I liked it better than playing the piano or going to parties. I had taught private school.

"But, Corabelle, these Indians need agriculture and animal husbandry, not German and dancing."

"My eyes haven't been shut when we were living on the farm. I have never plowed, but I know how. I could teach them how."

"I was reading the other day that the temperature out there often drops to fifty or more below. Child, how could you stand such cold?"

"Put on more clothes."

Father got up and paced about. Restlessly he

rubbed his hands together. "Well, if you are determined—anybody with such determination——"

I didn't wait for the actual words of consent. I
ran to find Mother. That she was the mainspring
of Father's life I had long known. I could see how
he had escaped to his beloved farms for short stays,
but had always returned to the cities for the long
periods. But as for me, I had no fear of Mother's
kind of argument. I went in saying to myself
that I didn't care how hard she cried. Marian
was with her, sewing, trying to finish a black satin
dress for the tea tomorrow. Marian looked up and
frowned as I came in. She had been telling me
often of late that she thought the reason that I
wanted to teach Indians was so that I might become
"more outrageously forward" than I now was.

"Mamma, Papa has just said that I could——"
I blurted out without ceremony.

Mamma broke in with, "Don't tell me, Corabelle, that you came here just to foist some more
of this Indian talk on me. I'll not endure it!"

"Then I'll have to go without your consent,
if——"

"How supremely ridiculous! You, a girl brought
up and educated as you have been among cultured
people, you, teaching those disgusting Indians!
How do you propose to go?"

"I thought you and Papa might not be able to
afford it, so I have told the church, and they——"

"Church? What church?"

"The Presbyterian on Avenue C."

I might just as well have exploded a cannon in Mother's face. She was an Episcopalian. After my love affair, she had humored me by permitting me to attend the Avenue C Presbyterian Church where I taught my private school. In Illinois I had attended the Baptist Church with Eleanor Eggleston, the ward right out of E.D.E.N. Southworth's books, whose wealthy guardian had married her.

"She just wants to get away from you and Papa so you can't control her," Marian said, attempting to comfort our hysterically weeping mother. "Don't cry, Mamma."

Mother recovered herself enough to sob, "Corabelle, why, just anybody knows that Indians are in a different class. Really, Corabelle, Indians are never admitted into the best society."

"John A. Logan has been with Indians," I shot back, "and, besides, it won't make me an Indian just to teach them." Mother had always taken particular pride in being included in the Logan guest lists.

"And so you intend to waste all your bringing up on these wild people? Heavens! Corabelle, why are you so blind and stubborn?"

"I have learned to work," I began, and added the explanation about my service as maid. Mother

Corabelle Fellows' Father, Homer Fellows

Corabelle Fellows' Mother

Corabelle Fellows' Sister Marian

dropped her sewing. Marian ran to her. But I went on, untouched by the stricken pallor of my mother's face. "I can sew and darn. I have taught private school and I know many subjects well enough to teach them. I can teach music, history, astronomy——" On and on I raced, omitting nothing.

Mother sank back, very pale, and resumed her work. "Corabelle Fellows," she enunciated in her chilliest manner, "go, if you must, but don't insult my ears with another word about your loathsome Indians! You'll be back in a week."

I raced to the minister's house to tell him, raced back to pack feverishly. But I did not sleep that night.

Next morning I resumed my precipitous preparation for departure. Mother, dry-eyed and very erect, came up to my room to bring me a little flatiron. "I hope that even in that outlandish place you will remember to keep your clothes pressed," she said. I still have that little flatiron. In retrospect I have sometimes felt sorry for Mother when I looked at it—the symbol of that nicety of life she valued above all else and could not persuade me to value at all. I took the board from my easel and added that to my pile of things to take. I told myself it would be a good lapboard for writing letters, but I knew also that I must take some memento of the painting that I loved so well. Fifty-three years later, when I was using it to dry peaches, it cracked in two in my coal-heated oven.

The day before I left, Mother came slowly up the stairs. She carried a pair of rough high boots. She set them down. "You'll be having pneumonia, first thing you know, with that cough of yours, Corabelle———" Hastily she left the room.

My trunk had been the gift of the church, and they had half filled it with blankets, leggings, and sweaters. It was hard getting into it all that I wanted to take, but at last the lid was closed and locked securely in place. In my closet still hung all my gay and pretty dresses, and, covered carefully against dust, my coming-out gown. In March Mother had sought to restore me to my senses by giving me a coming-out party, topped off by attending the inaugural ball of President Garfield. In a changeable silk taffeta gown, puffed and ruffled from sixteen yards of silk, and distended with hoops and many handmade petticoats, I had danced beneath the glass-prismed chandeliers in my first formal gown. It surely had been pleasant. I had not lacked for beaux. The music, the gleaming floor, the flowers, I can still recall with a kind of glow—and I am seventy-six. That I had been away to school was sufficient excuse for a coming-out party for a girl of twenty.

Now, the last day of October, the date agreed upon for my departure, was here. I left my pretty dresses with scarcely a second thought. Soberly clad, feeling a weighty responsibility, I went out from my girlhood home forever. I was accompanied to the station by all of the family. That morning old Kate, who had come back to Washington with us from the Virginia farm, had followed me up-stairs to make a last plea. Since the decision that I was to go had been made, Kate had never ceased to eye me continually and tearfully. Now she flung her old arms about me and moaned, "O Mis' Coah! Doan go! Doan! Day sho' gwine kill y'." I, completely off guard by the unexpectedness of her outburst, assured and assured that there was not the least danger, but I shed my first brimming tears there in old Kate's comforting and loving embrace.

I can see their faces yet as they stood watching the train move off: Father as near to crying as I had ever seen him, except when little Clement died; Mother and Marian, very chic and modish, very shocked, and a little sorry to lose me. But old Kate shuffled from one misshapen foot to the other in the extremity of her grief, and wailed mightily, as one might for the dead. It was the last time we were all together.

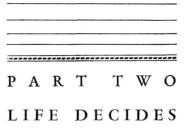

PART TWO

LIFE DECIDES

Excepting when I slept, which was very little, I cried almost all of the entire way from Washington, D. C., to Springfield, Dakota, then a territory. Among my luggage was a square box of lunch—chicken-pimento sandwiches, chocolate layer cake, grapes, pears, and apples. Several times I tried to eat some of it, but the sight and odor of it would bring back my mother's kitchen, and the tears would fall faster than before. I would retie the string and return the box to its place.

The second day an old woman walked casually past my seat where I sat sniffling. "If you have brought lunch, too," she said in the most matter-of-fact way, "suppose we two eat together."

I gulped. She took this to mean that I was delighted, not so far from the actual fact. She settled her well-upholstered person beside me, and once more I untied the string on the lunch box. What with eating her own lunch with definite relish and with passing bright and impersonal comments upon everything excepting home and friends, she managed to aid me to eat—a little.

As we neared the end of the journey I gradually achieved a calmer mind and a less swollen face. I tried to imagine what this place *would* be like to which I was going. The long train which I had boarded at Washington had switched off one coach after another until now but a single coach remained, a coach bearing four passengers—three men and myself. The sympathetic conductor stopped to say we were not far from Springfield. The country grew more and more desolate. The train moved slower and slower. It barely crawled. We were hours late.

The youngest of the three men asked my destination. His eyebrows lifted a trifle when I answered "Springfield," and he warned me against hotels. "But there is a little boarding place a little way up on Main Street due west of the depot on the left-hand side," he offered.

At long last the train stopped. I stepped down onto a wooden platform in Springfield, Dakota, into the most penetrating cold I had ever experienced. Everything was still, the platform deserted. A little town of a few hundred low houses spread indistinctly beneath the sharp, cold stars. As I stood, hesitating, shivering, two half-grown Indian boys came racing breathlessly around the corner of the station house, a low ten-by-fifteen structure.

I understood well enough from their pantomime and an occasional English word that they had been sent to take me to Riggs's School, my destination. But what was this they were repeating, both singly and in unison: "No cross, day cross!" They said it over and over.

The station agent came out. "Ferry's not runnin' 'count uv ice in t' river. Hafta wait till mornin'," he said briskly, and returned quickly out of the cold into his dimly lit room.

I remembered the information of the young man on the train. I started up the main street with the two boys, who were much relieved and very cheerful, tagging after me. I tried to talk to them. I had heard about their chief, or some chief—Gray Bear —or was it Black Bear?

Immediately they became sullen. "Perhaps," mumbled one of them. He looked at me suspiciously.

"Is your chief here?"

"Perhaps."

"He is my friend," I ventured.

They thawed as suddenly as they had frozen. In turn they grasped my hand and wrung it painfully, over and over again, with, "How, my friend! How, my friend!" Later I learned that the Sioux Indian resented inquiry, especially concerning friend or family, unless the questioner first established his own friendship to the one inquired about. "Perhaps" is their invariable reply, a reply which reveals nothing at all.

The boys went on when I stopped before the door

of a little wooden building that showed no light. I
rapped several times before I heard a hopeful noise
within. The door was finally opened a third of the
way by a wooden man whose face bore no expre-
sion of any kind. When I asked for lodging he
opened the door another lap to let me enter. But
he didn't speak.

I asked for food.

"Supper's done," he said.

"But I haven't eaten. Just give me a little left-
over food and something warm to drink."

He did. I tried, but I was unable to eat what he
set out on the bare table beside the kerosene lamp:
a dab of cold bread pudding, a dab of butter, a slice
of very soggy bread, a huge heavy cup of warmed-
over, lukewarm, very strong tea.

Then he led me up to a bare and stingingly cold
room. I did not sleep. The intense quiet of the
house and of the town outside—I opened a window
and stuck my head out for a better view—the fact
that I was hungry for the first time in my life—
these things so frightened and desolated me that
I cried until morning under the smelly bedclothes.
Home seemed at the end of the world. How glad
I was that Mother and Marian couldn't see me!

Next morning the two boys appeared and escort-
ed me, with many a grin and "How, my friend" to
the bank of the muddiest river I had ever seen, the
Missouri. It was choked with dirty ice. Here their

canoe waited. I was in an agony of fright, paralyzed past moving so much as a finger, all the way over. The boys seemed to miss death by a hairsbreadth at every stroke of the paddle. All the way up, all the way down, over on one side, over on the other, went the canoe, dodging back and forth between the cracking, jamming ice with breathtaking agility.

They brought up the canoe on the shore and sprang out easily. Then I was treated to the hardest handshaking yet. This time the boys grunted prodigiously in approval, in addition to nearly breaking my arm. It seemed that since I had sat still—as a good squaw should—and had not tried to talk, I had won their respect!

During the remainder of the trip I sat on the open seat of a spring wagon drawn by two ponies. Over a rutted trail we went, up and down interminable hills, mile after mile. It was late evening when, with returning hope, I made out a group of low buildings etched sharply against dun-colored grass. They were the first dwellings sighted since leaving Springfield.

I was numb with cold. I climbed stiffly down over the wheel, unaided, to be received by a somber woman of spare person and brief speech. Mrs. Riggs's black hair was combed down sleek and straight and badgered into a hard knot upon the back of her head. "Well, good evening," she said.

The group of buildings stood out bluish white against the bleak brilliance of the chill sunset: a little chapel with a very tall spire, four cottages, two rather large buildings, square and unadorned —all of them of wood. I shivered.

"Come in," said Mrs. Riggs.

When she had led me through her savory kitchen, through a large living room with a bow window filled with blooming plants, up rag-carpeted stairs and into my room with its bright fire and snowy counterpane and curtains, I saw that this woman was nothing short of an angel. "Supper will be ready in fifteen minutes," she said, clipping each word short, and went out. I both ate and slept— without weeping—that first night at Riggs's.

Next morning I was promptly put to work. Mr. Riggs led the way to a classroom where he opened the door upon fifteen little Indian girls—very little girls—from five to eight, I judged. "Teach them to sew," he said, and shut the door.

They knew but little English. I knew no Sioux. But I could show them how.   I remembered what I had said to my father. I took each docile brown little hand in mine and guided it to set fine hemming stitches in the squares of purple, orange, blue, and scarlet calico which they held. They sat in a circle upon little chairs and turned their large, bright black eyes upon me unblinkingly. There was not a sound. Then one of them turned and whispered

Mrs. Riggs

Young Men's Hall at Riggs's School

The Riggs Residence

The Little Boys' Cottage at Riggs's School

something to her neighbor. This tattler ruthlessly called out in a virtuous voice the horrifying news that "Maggie she talka Dakota." The children had been duly impressed with the rule that only English was to be spoken. Now the culprit stitched on while the rest looked questioningly at me. "We will all try to speak English only," I said. It became deadly still again while little heads bent to the task of learning to sew the white man's way.

A few days after my arrival I went out on the grounds for a walk. I was at once joined by several Indian girls of about my own age. They took turns being my walking partner. They fingered my dress, my sweater, my hair, my shoes. When I could stand it no longer I suggested that we sit down and talk awhile—in English.

"Ugh."—a decided negative.

I insisted. "What is your name?" I heard, and looked around to find that a tall handsome girl with a purple seal upon her forehead had spoken. I walked back to her, saying, "My name is Corabelle."

"Ugh! Ugh!"—this time a disgusted negative followed by a rapid-fire exchange of comment in Sioux.

"What does it have of meaning?"—again the girl at my side.

"Core means girl, and belle, beautiful," I said,

grateful that my language training had made it possible for me to answer promptly.

"That is not good—is not right"—this time from another girl.

"Do you like Indian?"—this from a third girl.

"Oh, yes, indeed," I said unctuously, "that is why I have come."

"Ha! Good! Good!"—a chorus now.

"You want name of good meaning?" asked the girl with the seal.

"Yes, indeed!" I answered, nodding enthusiastically.

She turned me about as if she feared I might break and looked long and closely into my eyes. "Wichipitowan!" was her verdict.

The girls broke out in an animated chorus, "Wichipitowan! Wichipitowan!"

"What does it have of meaning?" I asked, much to their merriment.

"Blue Star."

Thus was I rechristened there in the late afternoon in the biting cold on Riggs's campus. I bore the name Blue Star longer than Corabelle. Everybody found it more suitable, for, though I was none too pretty, my eyes were very blue, indeed.

When I asked the other teachers that evening about the purple seal they told me that was the mark of the chief's daughter.

I soon swung into the program at this place. I

The Girls Who Rechristened Corabelle Fellows "Wichipitowan" ("Blue Star")

had a class in arithmetic for these girls who had given me the "right" name, and one also for the older boys. I had my class of little seamstresses, and a class in geography for the big boys, besides meeting these older students in the auditorium each night to teach them—of all things—etiquette! I wrote my mother this. She was definitely rejoiced and comforted. In the auditorium after etiquette class I taught them to play charades, drop the handkerchief, and clap in and clap out. While I played the piano they sang both Sioux and English songs. "This language training might turn out to be an asset," Mother wrote.

Almost every evening I had visitors, in twos and threes—the Sioux rarely go alone. Blame and praise are thus equally divided—especially blame. This custom also foils the gossip who would question of private affairs of one from another. There was no thought of impropriety. The girls came for lesson help usually, for they were more studious and responsible about lesson preparation than the boys. The boys usually wanted to play dominoes. Almost noiselessly they would appear at my door.

"*Can skata?*" (wood for play) they would ask, hopefully.

"How about lessons?"

"Ugh!" with a decided headshake. "*Can skata?*"

They would come in then and play rapidly, counting up gains with a speed that little resembled class answering. They never made loud noise and never boasted. The winner was content to celebrate with a single brief smile. I gave them hot coffee before they left, and they became my willing slaves and never tired of saying—for they were mightily impressed with my learning—*"Wichipitowan lila ota."* ("Blue Star knows much.")

The girls would study, finger my clothes, and drink coffee. They doted on me, and I became very fond of them. They loved to hear me tell of a city and what it is like. Here I used my training in drawing, to aid words, and thereby became doubly marvelous in their estimation. The girls wanted me to wear a gray wool dress with red collar and cuffs all the time. It was cut on straight lines and had a long red girdle ending in tassels. It was the one dress I owned that bore some similarity to their clothing. My gray skirt and middy blouses worried them terribly; thus to cut my altitude into two distinct zones was a manner of dress they found uncanny. My hair was very heavy and much below my waist. They wanted me to ask Mr. Riggs to let me wear it as they did theirs, in plaits brought to the front over the shoulders and hanging loose.

The boys, particularly, were astonishingly quick in geography. The day I explained to them the extent of territory in the United States and told them of the towns and cities it held, their marveling faces were a sight not to be forgotten. But when

I turned the map over, disclosing this same United States set in its niche in a world map, they grew noisy with their *"Wichipitowan lila ota."* After that I walked among them as a goddess.

The older girls outshone the boys in arithmetic. They never ceased to be openly pleased when the problem proved out. Mr. Riggs had taught them rudiments. During the seven months in which I taught them they became proficient in long and short division, denominate numbers, and fractions. I had no trouble with the little girls or the older boys, and only once with the older girls. That was during my first week. Mr. Riggs had warned me to "show them who was boss" right from the outset.

I asked one of the girls to put a problem on the board. She sat stolidly. I repeated the request. She still sat. I scarcely knew what to do. I weighed one hundred and ten, she perhaps sixty pounds more. I went on assigning problems until every other girl was working at the board. Still I could not think what to do. Then it came to me. I rose suddenly, purposely letting the book in my lap crash to the floor. I reached the girl while she was still mobile from surprise. I seized her shoulders and shook her with all my might. "Blue Star has a strong heart," she said, and rose and went to the board. Fifty years later when I returned to view the scenes of my youth once more before my fading vision should make it impossible, we two laughed together over

that shaking. She was an old woman, as was I. She
had sight in but one eye, and I was losing sight in
both, but we laughed over the memory, and could
both give the figures of that problem in long
division.

The Indian children were all most anxious to be
noticed. *"He Mye"* ("This is I") was their constant phrase. It was their way of showing that they
could answer the question, that they wanted to be
invited to my room, that they were standing at my
desk and wanted me to acknowledge their value and
presence. The smallest girls were a constant delight.
I marveled at their patience and ability in sewing.
Before the year was out they were making all manner of undergarments.

One day one of them came to me and furtively
asked me for *"wasena."* I questioned her and found
that this, the favorite dish of the Sioux, is made of
bone marrow, pounded with cherry pits and cherries and lean meat. I wrote a letter or two, and
when the delicacy finally came from her home she
shared it with me. I found it excellent food. These
children would sigh, when pleased or impatient or
disappointed, just as their elders sighed. The little
sewers never returned a word when a seam must be
ripped and done over—they only sighed, a weary,
long-drawn sigh. I remember some of their English
names given them by the school: Rose Cordier,
Lucy Medicine Man, and Nancy Kitto.

At Riggs's I was happy to have a pony to ride. From the burro days of the Missouri farm and the horseback days in Virginia I had acquired some skill in riding. My mount here was a sorrel pony that one of the boys would bring to the hitching rack for me. The first time I saw it my memory raced back to another sorrel pony, the property of one Orlando Bullock, who, proud beyond words at being the owner of a "cowboy pony" brought to him from Texas by a doting uncle, had ridden the animal to school where, from among all of the girls, I, alone, had been invited to "ride behind me a piece." When I had gained my seat the young smart aleck had reared the pony until I had had to grab him about the waist to keep from being sent spinning. I held tightly enough, but I never let him call me his "girl" again, and didn't so much as speak to him. I had many a canter on the tough little pony at the Riggs's school. He was both gentle and willing, but I never mounted him that I could not in memory hear the derisive calls of the other children when my childhood swain had forced me to embrace him publicly, "Oh, look at Corabelle, looky, looky!"

One evening a short time after my arrival at Riggs's I was called down into the parlor to meet a party of parents of my pupils who had come in from some of the distant villages. There were only men in the group. They had asked to see the new teacher. When I entered the room one great fellow spoke, "*He tue?*" ("Whoever can this be?").

Mr. Riggs said, "This is Miss Fellows, our new teacher."

To a man they grunted with supreme contempt, accompanied by profound headshakings.

"*Huh! Takua cinstina!* ("Oh, gracious! She is too little!").

Not yet knowing their language, I bowed and smiled graciously. Innocently I remained in the room, but was altogether shunned by the guests. I must confess I was somewhat terrorized when the men produced their long pipes, each ornamented with scalp locks. Most of these locks were black shining Indian hair, but there was a curly yellow lock upon the pipe of the fellow who had led in the disgust over my size.

When spring opened, the prairie became a veritable miracle to me. As far as one could see nodded pink and purple, blue and red, yellow and white bloom in the fresh green grass. I was particularly taken by the small globular cacti, and one of the other teachers and I decided to try transplanting some of them to bring into the schoolrooms. Armed with kitchen knives and small baskets, we set out. We wandered from plant to plant, led by the lure of seeing what seemed a more brilliant flower a little farther on. Suddenly a violent neighing and thudding of hoofs made us look up. A great herd of

wild ponies was dashing down upon us. In the lead
was a glossy black stallion, his long mane and heavy
tail blown out by the wind. As we looked he reared
upon his hind legs, and came prancing on, just
upon those two legs. His teeth were bared, and he
emitted a noise like the high-pitched shriek of a
woman. Terrorized, we dropped flowers, baskets,
and knives and ran as fast as fear would let us.
We were able to roll uncermoniously under the
wire guard fence just as the beautiful maddened
little beast reached it. We ran on and made the
second fence before we turned to watch the pawing herd. Their neighing was horrid. As I stood
watching them, I remembered a Chillicothe experience when one day I had decided to observe at close
range the dirt-pawing operations of Cox's bull.
He, further maddened by the scarlet of my calico
dress, had hurled himself, bellowing, after me. He
threw himself with such a heavy impact against
the fence that I had just crawled under that he was
thrown to his knees as the fence post cracked off
at the ground. I wrote home about the wild ponies.
I remember the very words of Mother's reply:
"Certainly in that heathenish place you will be
destroyed, if not by Indians, surely by the wild
creatures."

The Sioux were inveterate gumchewers. They
manufactured the gum from the juice of the purple coneflower. They collected this patiently, go-

ing from flower to flower, slashing the stem and catching the dripping juice in a pottery bowl or jar. When the liquid was boiled down, the residue was a fine, rubberlike substance, very durable, which all of them chewed almost constantly. The men chewed with much noise and swagger; the girls were experts at snapping it. I never met a Sioux with the toothache, perhaps their gum chewing explains why.

I do not know that they used any other flower. The coneflowers were plentiful, mostly purple, though some were yellow. There were sensitive roses, a tiny morning-glorylike flower—the bindweed—buffalo peas, and white and yellow prickly poppies. Meadow larks and prairie hens were everywhere, and there were robins and jays.

Before I ended my apprenticeship—I was at Riggs's to become acclimated and to learn the Sioux language—I grew to love the older girls. They admitted me to their hair pluckings when they removed any luckless hair from the half-inch-wide partings on their heads that ran from forehead to nape. Then they painted the part with brilliant red paint. They complained because the school would not permit them to paint their fingernails, too. At home, they told me, they used the red or yellow paint, sometimes both at once and on the same hand. They were angry because they were obliged to bathe in winter. Oil kept out cold, they asserted, and if you were obliged to wash off the oil every day, why shouldn't you feel cold all of the time. We rode and walked and talked together and exchanged information and ideas upon such momentous questions as the cut of dresses—and scalp locks—and how to stay on the sled if Mr. Fred Riggs, home from school in midwinter, was trying to spill you.

I never became acquainted with Mrs. Riggs. My youthful enthusiasm seemed to act on her like a violent poison. The only times when she unbent towards me—then only just perceptibly—was when I praised her flowers or cooking or housekeeping. Her flowers were the one bright spot that winter in a waste of snowbound prairie. "I have my house to keep," was her invariable remark. "Mr. Riggs tends to the rest."

I had studied the Sioux tongue a part of every day under Mr. Riggs; and now that spring was here and I could make myself understood, it was decided that I should go on to a less civilized center, Oahi, where Mr. Riggs's brother, Thomas, was in charge. On the day before the one set for my departure, I was looking out of the window of my room, terrified to see low-rolling and green-fringed clouds that appeared to be coming on at a terrific pace. I closed the window hastily, wishing they had not removed the double windows the day before. Those windows had been friendly all winter,

cutting the keen northwest blasts and giving a
sense of snug protection. I fled precipitously down
the stairs. Mrs. Riggs was calmly laying the table
for the evening meal. She placed each piece with
the same meticulous care as always, and did not
look up.

"Oh, Mrs. Riggs, I think it's a cyclone!" I
shouted in distress.

Mrs. Riggs made no response. She made no pause
in her silver laying.

"It's just awful and it's coming so fast——"

"It is not coming here."

"Oh, it will tear everything to pieces and
kill——"

Mrs. Riggs walked slowly to the cupboard for
the plates. She picked them up, came back to the
table. At last she turned and looked at me.

"Did you never see a cyclone?" she asked. Her
tone was cool, edged with contempt.

I shook from head to foot. The storm came on.
The air was deathly still and had grown hot suddenly. Mrs. Riggs laid the plates and disappeared
into her kitchen where I heard her spoon in a calm
rhythm against the bottom of the saucepan as she
stirred—probably a dressing for the pudding. She
was right. The cyclone didn't hit us, but it hit
the next settlement and wrought death and havoc
for a hundred miles.

Next day I said good-by to my pupils and the

others. As I came down from my clean, cheerful room past the bow window of flowers and out into the kitchen, Mrs. Riggs glanced up from her dish washing. "Well, good-by," she said.

CHAPTER FIVE

Mr. RIGGS told me in parting that I would find rougher Indians who spoke a different dialect of Sioux than that I had learned from him. He had taught me Santee Sioux. Now I was to encounter the Teton Sioux. Riggs's had been wild enough in its surrounding country, but the coach, a four-horse, mud-spattered affair, was rolling about on what appeared to me to be a trailless and endless plain. I rolled about with the coach and longed for pillows to ease my contacts with the sides of the vehicle when, missing falling over by some miracle, the driver would right his coach and I would find myself thrown violently across the seat. It was night when a weary and battered young person looked out at one of the frequent stops to see a low and commodious log house, just as a plump, smiling little woman threw open the door and came running down the path. I loved her at sight. She helped me down and squeezed my hand and kissed me heartily. "Come right in, dear. How tired you must be," she said, her arm about me as we climbed the path. "Everything's right on the table." I knew I was going to be happy here.

I took a review of myself that night. Of the seven teachers who had started with me at Riggs's, just a Miss Illsley and I had held out and remained. The others had left for warmer latitudes. Of my pay, six hundred dollars, paid quarterly, I had, at my father's suggestion, a quarter of it in a savings account in a Washington bank. I read and reread all of my letters from home. I wrote a long letter to Mother. I told how I had taught Indian boys and young men to darn socks and underwear. But I didn't tell her how I had said to one strapping brave, "Here are some socks to darn," and he had answered menacingly, "What bad thing is this for a brave to do? That is for women. Do it yourself."

I had laid his work over his knee and left the room, and he had it done when I returned. I told her I had had a happy birthday and had been given a cake and a napkin ring. But I didn't tell her how I had called the little boys together and with much yelling and beating on tin cans and waving the two school flags, I had led them in a procession several times around the school grounds, bringing up at Mr. Riggs's door, where, to my utter shame, he had come out and upbraided me without stint. I had had difficulty in convincing him that it was my own birthday I was celebrating and not the election of a President—of a political party of which Mr. Riggs

was the bitter enemy! I reported how much money
I had saved, but made no mention of eating canned
sweet potatoes at fifty cents the half pint tin from
the agency store. I recorded Mrs. Riggs's fine
housewifery, but omitted the cyclone. I enclosed
some arithmetic problems done by my class of
girls, but I reserved the story about shaking Lucy.
I told of Mrs. Riggs's good food, but didn't say
anything about the dreadful "dining hall" where
pupils and teachers ate, nor that I had been dreadfully hungry many, many times. I described my new
fur leggings, but quoted no forty-below figures.
I wrote of the dainty room I had had and of the
culture of the other teachers but left out a description of how I bathed and deloused very dirty
and smelly little Indian boys. I said nothing about
six other teachers who had been unable to stand
the cold, the food, the Sioux language, and the
magnificent odors.

Next day I entered upon my duties at this new
center, so much ruder and smaller than Riggs's.
My only teaching was as assistant in sewing. I was
to visit among the tepees which scattered about in
all directions, four or five together. I wondered
how to do it. Here was quite a different situation
than shaking a young woman into doing a problem
in long division, with a stern principal across the
hall to aid in bringing action if necessary. I looked
about my room and collected a few trinkets, a pin-

cushion, a dresser scarf, and a small and beribboned
soiled-handkerchief bag. They were all the loving
labor of some missionary society somewhere and
had come to me via the missionary barrel. I set out
on foot.

No one was at home at the first tepee, but the
next one was crowded. At my approach every face
showed no small degree of uncertainty, ranging
from intense surprise to last-minute glance before
fleeing. I hastened to say I had come to visit, and
told them who I was. "Visit" proved to be the magic
word. They welcomed me and welcomed me. I
sat down on the bare ground, worn grassless for
quite a space about the tepee entrance, and opened
my bag. They flocked around me.

"To trade," I said, in brief English accompanied
by pantomime.

The pantomime was wholly unnecessary. I had
so many offers I could not remember them. Many
from near-by tepees joined the buzzing crowd.
The soiled-handkerchief bag was the thing all of
them wanted most and bid for. It was of brilliant
and highly designed cretonne and was closed with
a bright red ribbon. The men particularly seemed
charmed with this kind of closing device, a sack
with a handle. They took turns strutting about
with this appointment for a lady's boudoir, on the
crook of the arm. After I had demonstrated the
use of pins, the pincushion filled with pins called

forth copious approving grunts from the squaws. They fingered—much to its permanent harm—the dresser scarf, done realistically in roses and forget-me-nots in brilliant silk floss.

My load was heavy and not to be compassed by a handbag on the trip back to my room. I had anklets, beads, pottery, a wooden knife and spoon, a beautiful foxskin. It wasn't long until my room began to look like a museum, so I left off trading and merely visited. Some of the things I sent home, the foxskin to Father. I still have his letter acknowledging it, a letter written in fine, exact script, so fine that those who read to me can scarcely make it out, so fine that one of his pages contains more words than a letter of Mother's and of Marian's together. He was richly pleased, for he wrote:

> Your present of a fine fox skin pleased me, indeed, It recalled to me the days of my youthful sporting—those happy and careless days—happiness seems to diminish with age. . . .

I sent a pipe also—without scalps—small potteries, beads, ornaments, and moccasins. These delighted Mother.

She began to realize that not even an Indian spends all of his time and cunning in killing missionaries. She wrote:

> They are strange and not at all what is being worn, but they seem to be comfortable, and the ornaments, some of them, are quite attractive. I am unable to learn by examination just how they do it.

I always had to compromise when I taught the Indian women sewing. A paper pattern was a miracle to them, but they refused absolutely to open a dress with buttons down the front. To them this was the pinnacle of immodesty. They made a closing from armpit to waist. They would have no fitted sleeves. Indian sleeves—loose, long, and voluminous—were sewed into dresses fashioned like those worn in Washington at that time. They never ceased to marvel over our fabrics. I found my traded dresser scarf far from its original owner, gracing a rude box-and-willow affair upon which the lady of the tepee kept her toilet articles. Now I wonder if my wily plan to interest these Indian women in the details of a white woman's private room was either wise or necessary. I invited them to visit me. I kept my room faultlessly. They came, they saw, they wanted—as I hoped they would. They would have walked ten miles through a blizzard just to see and feel a length of smooth, richly figured silk. The missionary ladies of those days would have been scandalized had they known upon whose shoulders some of their silk and woolen gifts finally rested—and rested grandly.

I came to a tepee one day just as food was about to be served. Indians had no regular mealtime, that activity being determined by who happened to be at home. This, in turn, rested upon work to be done. Herds, wood, water—and visiting—must come first. If all these had been attended to and there was food, and it was cooked—then the family ate. All conditions had been fulfilled on this day of my call, and I was asked to dine. I had read of how the Indian squaw waited until her acceptedly superior mate had had his fill, he and his grown sons with him; so I accepted, not only because my long walk had given me a not too particular appetite, but also because I wanted to learn more of their customs.

In the center of a tanned buffalo hide, placed hair side down upon the dirt floor of the tepee, the woman set down a great earthen pot which she carried, unaided, from the fire. The family disposed themselves about the skin, picnic-fashion, the men and boys cross-legged, the women and girls with both feet stretched out to the left side. I watched them and followed their etiquette. The wife, with a very long-handled fork, now distributed the rations. I have a yellowed and incomplete old paper written with a lead pencil in which I had started to describe this meal for a church paper. I quote from it:

> The feast of meat—I hope it was not dog-meat—was forked from the steaming pot into the hands of the consumer. There was also "Dakota bread," black, dirty-looking stuff, fried like doughnuts in fat. There was also squash baked in the shell. The eating was accomplished with neither plate nor fork but directly from the hand. All sat down together, mother, father, children and grandchildren. Before I left they had the littlest girl named Pte' (Little Calf) dance the Da-

kota feast-dance for me. It seemed ludicrous to me but the child did not smile once but went through the long dance as sober as a deacon. She was not more than four. . . .

They had seen me coming from a distance and had done everything they thought would please me. The father had come out part way to meet me, while his wife had hurried inside to get out the finest skin and place it in the seat of honor for me. With great pride I was shown the dogs and pigeons, the wood piled in readiness for winter—all sufficient proof that he was not lazy. With rhythmic head and arm he showed me how hard he had worked. Just as I entered the mud-lined lodge I caught a glimpse of one of the older girls washing the baby's face!

I returned to Oahi across the autumn prairie. The sun sank, and I heard the nighthawk's click. I had no thought of fear, but walked on alone across the level grasslands and arrived home to find that the mail had come. Hungrily I took the letters to my room, where I devoured every word of them.

There were ten of them. My cousin, Ann Haight, from Macgregor, Iowa, wrote glowingly about her approaching marriage, "I'm on the river as late as I please with C and nobody says anything about it since I'm engaged."

My friend, Marian Hubbard, wrote from Mt. Holyoke College:

Mrs. Riggs from the Santee station was in the ironing room this morning. . . . I have learned to count in Indian, I practice it when I button my shoes. . . . How lonely you must be! Don't your heart ever fail you? I am so homesick here, how must you be there in Dakota? O, why did I ever leave home? Rules are so strict, we haven't been out after six for six weeks. How I do long for a moonlight walk! I believe I'd like to teach Indians in Dakota, too, only it's three years until I graduate. Dear! This is only October, how can I stand it? But our room isn't so bare since we got up our screens and nick-nacks. . . ."

Lou Wilcox, who kept the half-price bookshop at 207 ½ Pennsylvania Avenue in Washington, said, "So Indians can write!" And there was one from Mother: "Just finished a new steel-gray silk with black trimmings to wear to a tea Mayme Richards and Mrs. Haws give tomorrow." And from Father: "I can't help worrying because you are alone. I do hope you will guard against trouble, for you are so far away I could not help you in time of need."

I really was more than a little lonely that night —and many other times. I suppose that it why when a trio of little Indian boys tapped at my door offering me a porcupine—to buy—that I put a dollar in each of three little brown hands. Much unappreciated and loving labor I spent on "Sharpy." He was not old enough to leave quills in my hands, but he did pace night and day around my room, close to the wall, in stoical and starving aloofness until I had to part with him. I traded Sharpy. The Indian women who got him confined him. As soon as a quill would appear she took it. Poor Sharpy! The Sioux valued porcupine quills next to purple calico. From them they made all manner of designs, combining them with beads.

First they were softened enough to be bent. With bone needle and sinew thread they were sewn securely into the pattern that had been previously designed. To please the women I attempted to learn the art, but the quills were only stubborn in my fingers, and the needle was so clumsy—seven inches long—that I did little but wound my fingers. They were amply disgusted with me and my weakness.

As I relate this I can see Sharpy, walking with bobbing tail, his inquisitive nose to the wall, pacing, slowly, slowly. I had offered him pumpkin and hardtack, corn and grass, but he had disdained them all. Before giving him up I had gone out to ask of the women just what to do to win his favor. They were quick to sense my situation. All anyone would say was *"Ma qu yi!"* ("Give him to me!") They had hurried in to bring forth their choicest things to trade. I got a fine foxskin and a pair of moccasins, and Sharpy was borne in triumph to her tepee by the winning bidder.

At Oahi I rode a spotted pony. The other teacher, Miss M., Mrs. Riggs, and the son, Theodore, all rode ponies, too. We often had riding parties. It took but a minute to run to the corral, strap on the saddle, and be off. Uncle Updegraff had sent me a fine red saddle which, however, was not a perfect fit for the pony. I tightened the girth and rode, anyway, becoming a little more skilled because the saddle was not oversecure. I was the envy of the whole country with a spotted pony and red saddle, for spotted mounts were coveted above all others. Eyes became very round with wonder when I described the factory where the saddle had been made and told them of the relative who had sent it—a man who sat under the same roof with the Great White Father at Washington and helped make laws at his council.

These people called me "Little Blue Star" and never ceased to marvel at my diminutive figure. I was five one, and weighed around a hundred. I rode daily and soon became used to following the trails alone. This, too, won me great praise. I had that most prized of all Indian qualities, "the brave heart."

CHAPTER   SIX

DURING this first sum-
mer at Oahi I learned, bit by bit, the whole gamut
of the lives of these Indians from birth to death.
In every tepee I entered I noticed that the occu-
pants, the furnishings, the fire—all were to be
found in exactly the same spot in every one of
them. By degrees I learned why. The women were
reticent and disliked questions. One, however,
seemed to take my questions as complimentary
and told me what I asked.

Back as far as anybody's grandmothers can remember, she said, the tepee must be thus: Directly
opposite the entrance, on the far side, shall be the
seat for the man. He must sit here, for it is he
who guards the rest and he must be first to see
approaching danger. His weapons and hunting
knives must hang just inside the door where he
may be able to snatch them up in haste. The wife
sits inside the door, her back to the opening, for
she is to be unconcerned with protection. She must
be busy at tending fire, stitching clothing, cooking
food. In most of the tepees at Oahi bows and arrows, a tomahawk, and sometimes a battle club

hung inside the opening to the left. The battle club was oftenest a stout carved wooden club into the end of which a large flint had been inserted and secured by sinew. One club I saw was made of the thighbone of a buffalo, with a flint inserted the same way.

The boys must always sit to the left, and the daughters, with their mother, to the right of the opening. In school they would sit no other way. Fifty years later I attended a church at Oahi where the women all sat on the right side and the men on the left.

Upon the women's side of the tepee, next the central fire circle, must stand the utensils for preparing food. These Sioux and the Cheyennes whom I later knew kept their equipment in a basketlike affair made of willows.

Around the outer edge of the tepee, rolled neatly into skin coverings, as one might roll a bolt of cloth in paper, were piled the beds of the family, and the clothing. They occupied no usable space. Each person attended to his bed, spread his skins and blankets out at night and rolled them up in the morning. Each sleeper lay with his feet to the fire. Rarely did I find a disorderly tepee. The dogs came in, of course, and the dogs had fleas, so that the Indians suffered much from that cause. I have seen a squaw take the stir-stick from the pot and whack a sniffing dog soundly on the head with it, then return it to the stew directly, or perhaps give it a slap-dash rubbing against her dress out of deference to my presence.

The tepees were cozy and homelike, but dark on cloudy days. They were never drafty on the floor, for these Indians all made an extra flap which they sewed around the entire perimeter of the tepee's skin covering. Some two feet from the tepee, they dug a drainage trench, and the dirt from it was piled firmly upon this flap of skin, making it impossible for air to enter at the base of the tepee. The rain and melting snow, drained into the ditch, was carried to a lower level by a second carry-off ditch.

Always upon the men's side hung a deerskin pouch, beaded and ornamented with carved deer toes. It contained kinnikinnick, the pulverized middle bark of the dogwood tree. These Indians had not learned of tobacco. When they did, they merely sprinkled a bit of it upon their pipeful of kinnikinnick.

Men and women both worked at making pottery. Early in the spring I had watched one of them who seemed to be honored with my interest. He had brought reddish, moist clay in basketfuls and had dumped it just outside his door. Here he squatted, and with sure touch moulded the piles, bit by bit, into a great earthen jar nearly three feet high and almost as wide. I stood by, watching a

long time, and he became so completely absorbed
in his task that he seemed to have forgotten that I
was there. He patted, smoothed, added, took away,
until the jar was of a roughly symmetrical shape,
about three inches thick in every part. When I
came back next day the jar was gone. He had
buried it, he said.

Some weeks later I came upon him digging carefully. Slowly he unearthed the treasure and with
great care lifted and carried it on his shoulder to
his tepee. He must have fired it somehow, for
when I saw it again it had a new compactness and
texture. He was now oiling it with animal fat put
on with a little brush he had made of tiny pliable
twigs tied together and shaped a little by trimming.
He sat back on his heels often to contemplate his
work. When I praised its shape and glossiness, he
smiled, well pleased. He had made a very intricate
design covering nearly all the surface, and the oil
all but obscured it.

In a few days I found him carving in the design
by following his dim-colored tracings. It had been
four months since I had first seen him working at
his piles of wet clay. Now, in October, he was busy
with his little paint rocks—hollow rocks filled with
the most brilliant of green, orange, red, purple,
and black. I asked him how he had made these pig-
ments and complimented him warmly, but all the
response I got was "perhaps."

When the jar was quite finished it was a princely thing, for while the colors taken singly were gaudy, he had combined and proportioned them until the design was satisfyingly lovely. The jar was finished after about five months of work. I saw it afterwards at a wedding feast, heaped with wild grapes, and I have yet to see a more beautiful thing.

I often watched them at their hide curing. They lifted the dripping skin from its bath of ashes and water and pinned it out, tightly stretched to the ground with wooden pins. Day after day they would work at scraping the upper surface with sharp stones or pieces of wood. If the animal's hair was to remain on the hide, no ash bath was given. The scraping was laborious and painstaking, and the men rarely worked at it long at a time. They would run off, mount a pony to see to the herds, or go to an adjoining camp to hunt or visit. The women worked hour upon hour, patiently.

When the skin had been well scraped and dried in the sun, they painted it with oil, a colored oil, usually giving it several coats. Six to eight of such skins, stitched together with bone needles and sinew thread, the seams painted many times, were enough to cover the fourteen to sixteen tepee poles. Cow and buffalo hides went to make the tepee and leggings, but only deerskin was used for shirts.

The women made the garments and tepees. In cutting skins, not the tiniest piece was wasted. The

larger scraps were stitched together to make moccasins, and the smallest pieces became ornaments
for dress or tepee. Often days of work went into
a skin but a few inches across, beaded in perfectly
executed geometric design. The women took much
delight in this work and were wonderful designers
of patterns, both naturalistic and geometric. These
tiny bead-and-porcupine-quill-decorated patches,
usually circular, were stitched here and there with
infinite care to the outside of the tepee, or used as
ornaments on shirts and skirts.

With moccasins, waist-high leggings of leather,
and a soft deerskin shirt coming to the knee, men
wore a breechclout and a wide leather belt, richly
ornamented. For cold weather they wore a heavy
blanket about their shoulders and pulled it up over
the head for added protection. In the very coldest
season the hunters wore skin sacks pulled over their
hands. Sometimes the thermometer fell to more
than forty below.

The belt was invariably of buckskin, heavily
beaded and stitched with porcupine-quill motifs.
The men wore armlets, anklets, necklaces, and
chains or ornaments both above and below the knee,
and, on festive occasions, little bells obtained from
traders, or strands of metal discs which jingled
musically when they danced. Ordinarily they wore
a hawk's feather in their braided hair.

With the utmost precision the women would fit

a piece of leather about the leg, mark it, cut it, and seam it. The Indian woman rarely mended. She worked too well in the first place for seams to rip. She ornamented everything she made excepting her own calico dresses, which she considered all ornament. Her own garments were the same as the man's, except that she wore a cumbersome skirt, short front and back, and dragging at the sides, in addition to moccasins, leggings, shirt, belt, and blanket.

Children were clad like their elders, but wore little or no ornament, and never feathers. They seemed content to wait until they, too, should be grown and enter into the gorgeousness of dress of their parents.

The Government was attempting to introduce leather shoes among Indians. Some were issued to Oahi. The men, following the experiment of one of their number, cut each boot round and round, into fine strips, and from these strips braided what they considered extra-fine hunting lariats. These ropes, plaited from many strands of tough leather, were the strongest things I have ever seen. It was impossible for an animal to break them. The fellow who first cut up his boots was supremely disdainful of them. "Ugh, ugh, *wasté sne*," he reiterated when I said to him, "Why did you do it, White Eagle?" While I was at Oahi all of Uncle Sam's well-meant gifts designed to keep the red man's feet warm were turned into lariats and hobbles for cattle.

I do not know if the Indians learned lassoing from the cowboys or the cowboys from the Indians. I have seen cowboys perform since my Oahi experience, but never did I see a cowboy who could ride with such whirlwind speed or throw the noose about the neck of the quarry with such a singing lariat or such unerring aim.

Although I did not see a single white-eagle feather at Oahi, it was spoken of in a tone denoting particular and elevated significance, accompanied with knowing nods and winks that I never was able to translate.

I had much trouble with the children when schooltime came. In the schoolroom they clung to their blankets. I never did master the boys. With open contempt for my orders they folded their blankets into cushions and sat upon them. The girls finally learned to hang theirs in the cloakroom, but they never liked to. They were extremely modest and shy; a blanket was a ready refuge in which to hide a blushing face.

The women contrived all sorts of decorations for their garments. They slashed the lower edge of their deerskin dresses into deep, fine, even fringe to which they attached discs made from deer toes, tiny tufts of rabbit fur, or soft down feathers. They were lavish with ornament and filled their

necks, legs, and arms with strand upon strand of
carved claw or hoof beads, stone beads, shells, and
even colored stones. Like the men, they used paint
commonly. Fingernails and plucked hair part were
painted, and the chiefs' families added a purple tat-
tooed circle between the eyes.

Besides this adornment the men checkered their
foreheads with diagonally placed stripes of paint,
the longitudinal ones red and the transverse ones
yellow. Each cheek also bore a similar checkered
splotch. Both men and women wore their hair in
two plaited braids, to which they attached anything
which they considered attractive: lengths of brilliant calico, beaver fur, hair, chains of deer toes,
feathers, and rabbit fur. They oiled their hair,
their bodies, and their clothing. The smell of rancid oil in the schoolroom was often nauseating.

The women one day invited me to go with them
for beans. Not having the least idea what I was
accepting, I went, and spent a day I shall never
forget. It was late autumn, and frost had pretty
well seared the short grass which now lay in a dull
bronze and mottled gray-green pattern as far as
you could see. Counting myself, there were eight
women in the party, and three times as many children, of varying ages. We set out very early in the
morning and had walked perhaps three miles from
the village before the first childish shout announced
a find.

How could there be anything on this treeless,
bushless, gray waste, I wondered. But now a little
girl ran, screaming shrilly, followed by the rest.
There, on the crest of the next prairie swell, she
swooped down and, quick as a squirrel, was up
again and bounding back to her mother. I saw
her pour into the deerskin pouch her mother carried two handfuls of tiny white beans, hulled and
dried. Now other children were running and
screeching triumphantly bringing back handfuls
of beans to their mothers. Now the woman next
me stopped and, pushing aside a little pile of grass
and leaves, disclosed a diminutive hoard of beans.
I was too astonished to ask questions and felt that
I must still be asleep and dreaming, until, as the
morning wore on and we wandered farther and
farther from camp, I myself found a little mound
of leaves hiding dried and shelled white beans.

"How do they get there?" I asked the little boy
who ran up to watch me take my spoil. Then I
listened to a fairy story. With all the poetry of
Indian speech he told me how the little prairie mice
search and gather the wild beans and bring them
one at a time to their storing place. When the
store is large enough the little fellows cover it with
grass and leaves to prevent the birds from seeing
and eating their food. We had been stealing the
winter stores of hundreds of prairie mice.

We dug sweet potatoes that day, too—queer,

little, irregular potatoes, hard to wrest from the
packed prairie soil with the sharpened sticks and
stones the women had brought with them. No
one ate anything all day, except a nibble at some
of the smaller potatoes, yet not a child cried or
begged for food, although we walked many, many
miles.

When we at last turned back it must have been
midafternoon. Each woman had perhaps three
pounds of beans and a little larger quantity of potatoes. The journey home was made in silence until
we came in sight of the tepees. Then the children
ran shouting ahead to be joined by a pack of dogs
that came barking out to meet us. In 1922, when
I returned to Oahi, one of these children, now an
old woman, entertained me in her modern frame
home. She served beans that the prairie mice had
hoarded.

Oahi women gathered wild turnip, also. They
removed the tough black skin, sliced the turnip, and
strung the slices on sinew thread to dry. Afterwards they stored them in deerskin pouches.
Turnip thus prepared was their delicacy. The gracious hostess of the tepee was always proud if she
had her turnip bag well filled and could say, "*Tipic
ina ya cin?*" ("Would you care for turnip?")

Their name for sweet potato was equivalent to
"man of the earth." They used them sparingly.
In fact, all of these vegetables were used, as one

might use seasoning, in the meat stew which ordinarily filled the great pot over the fire. If there
were plenty of beans they were boiled in a separate
vessel with a little tallow.

The Sioux's favorite meat was deer, but they
had herds of cattle, and ate much beef. Hunters
brought in deer, bear, prairie chickens, quail, ducks,
and geese. They ate beaver, too, and relished particularly the flat, fat tail. Fat puppies were saved
for feasts. Badgers, eels, and prairie dogs were
served when nothing else was to be had. I never
saw them eat snakes, but I had two fat snakes
brought me as a gift by two students. I was terrified, and screamed. The two boys made off, dan-
gling the snakes between them across a pole, and
laughing uproariously.

"Good meat," one had said, as he offered the pole.

When I had started back with a scream, he too
had stepped back, surprised.

I had recovered myself to ask, "Oh, you don't
eat snakes, do you?"

He had assured me that they did. But I had had
to refuse the gift, and the two boys had gone off
laughing, whether at my stupidity at not liking
snake meat or whether at the success of their plan
to scare the teacher, I never knew.

None of these Indians owned guns, but all used
the primitive bow. The arrows were headed with
flint and winged with goose feathers. Hickory was

soaked until it could be bent, when it was staked to dry in a curved shape. From this bent stick the bow was fashioned and, more often than not, ornamented with a surface design carved carefully in intricate lines. With a bow so fashioned and with a flint-headed arrow I aimed at and killed a fleeing rabbit after I had been a pupil of one of the boys for a short time. I loved archery. The news of my prowess spread over the entire reservation. I became a marvel in the eyes of the women as well as the men. The old chief came to me with a well-rehearsed speech of praise which was copiously punctuated with "good woman," and "brave woman." I kept the bow and arrow for many years, and knew every flake on the arrowhead. As a farmer's wife near Mena, Arkansas, many years later, I was given its counterpart by my husband, who had plowed it up in the field.

I witnessed an almost unbelievable skill of the children while I was at Oahi.

"Like duck?" they had queried.

"Oh, yes, indeed," I had told them.

"Get duck" had been the cryptic answer. Motioning me to follow, they had led me to the river. Here, in a shallow by the shore, a covey of wild ducks were feeding leisurely and floating idly about. Like snakes, two of the children wriggled on their bellies through the tall marsh grass, scarcely ruffling it. Arrived at the water's edge, they lay perfectly quiet for some little time, then, with an outflashing arm, almost too quick to follow, one made a grab. His hand closed so tightly and suddenly about the neck of a duck that it made no sound. When the child laid it before me, it was dead. I could not believe my eyes. Yet the Riggses told me at the supper table that night that these children caught not only wild ducks and geese in this way, but fish as well.

At Oahi, too, I accompanied the women one day on an expedition after fruit. There was quite a variety to be had up and down the river and on the prairie: wild crab apples, cherries, grapes, plums, buffalo berries, strawberries, and Juneberries. The Sioux women preserved, without sugar, by scalding and mashing the fruit and drying it in the sun. They were fond of fruit, but saved it for the friendly feasts or for marriage and burial feasts.

With skin clothing, the laundry problem had not appeared. But the brilliant calico they loved so well offered serious problems in upkeep. They were having their first experience with it that year. One woman solved the difficulty—since the weather was growing colder—by putting each new dress on over the older, soiled ones. By spring she was wearing five different dresses. She went down to the river when it began to grow warm in the spring, walked in, removed the top dress, and washed it. One at a time she removed all but one dress, laundered each and spread it out to dry on the grassy bank. No Indian woman would disrobe completely outside of her tepee. She was visibly perplexed as to what to do. Finally she solved the difficulty by wading in up to her chin and washing the dress on herself, without removing it.

CHAPTER SEVEN

ONE evening, shortly be-
fore I left Oahi, the Riggses and I went out on our
ponies together to bring in the herd from the free-
range pasture. As they so often did, the cows had
wandered out of sight, and we rode out along the
river timber in search of them. We had almost giv-
en up finding them when we heard, close at hand,
the most awful noise that I had heard up to this
time. The cattle burst forth together, bellowing
in a high-pitched key that was both weird and
terrifying. As we hurried in their direction, sounds
of pawing hoofs added to the distress signals. We
rode as fast as we could in the trailless woods and
came out on a clearing, where a pack of timber
wolves were fighting over the body of a newly
killed two-year-old. They snarled and tore at the
carcass, some fifteen of them, while the herd stood
by at a little distance, pawing the earth and bellowing with rage.

Young Theodore Riggs gave his pony the word,
and by a sudden dash into the midst of the wolves,
who were all off guard, surprised them into flight by
his sudden appearance. They fled, noiselessly and at

full speed, into the near-by timber. I had never before seen these animals, though I had ridden and tramped hundreds of miles about the Oahi camp. I wrote home that night, but I decided to reserve my recital of cattle killers until the night's experience was old enough not to be too startling to my readers.

Now, since I had begun to understand the Indian personality somewhat and had grown accustomed to meeting them in their own homes, I was thought to be prepared to go to a yet more primitive place. When I wrote Father that I was now going into the Cheyenne territory he answered, complimenting me on my advance. He must have been quite chesty about me. The agent sent me on the letter he had written Father, and Father's answer. Father's letter read, in part:

> She has engaged herself to the Cheyenne Agency, seems to have a talent for managing Indians. When you write to her you will see for yourself what a small young girl of pluck can do. These schools—right at the home of the Indian—are doing more good for the country than all the soldiers in the army.

Mother wrote:

> Kate Updegraff writes that you might get sick, and goodness knows what calamity she can't conjure up that might, could, or would befall you. Indeed, I wish you would not be so concerned with the sayings and doings of these perfect strangers who can't even speak the King's English without murdering every other word. . . . We are having short-cake for dinner. Do you *ever* get *anything* nice to eat. . . .

Just before I left Oahi, I went one evening to watch Mastincha (rabbit-woman), the most skilled maker of moccasins. She had several sizes and pairs in construction, some which she had sewed from the tiniest of scraps. Beside her lay three or four bone punches and many sizes and kinds of soiled leather, carefully trimmed to various shapes, mostly geometrical. One, I noted with much surprise, was the shape of a Grecian urn. Many were bizarre and strange to my idea of design motifs. Patiently and with much evident enjoyment, she tried first one and then another of these "patterns" to the moccasins she was finishing. When at last she found the one that suited her she held the "pattern" to the moccasin and with her bone punch outlined its shape upon the moccasin with the most precise touch. When the chief motif of the design to be beaded was thus outlined she began the slow work of beading, after she had tried out several color combinations and had chosen the one she preferred.

About her, also, lay several motifs, beaded and completed. These she tried out on various moccasins, and when the effect pleased her she placed the beaded ornament inside the moccasin it was to adorn when she came to sewing. To please me she stitched one of these in place. With her punch she made holes very close together in the outer edge of the motif. Holding it in its chosen position, she now punched holes in the moccasin to match those

in the motif. With sinew thread she deftly and
with incredible swiftness threaded the sinew back
and forth through the matched holes with her fingers, and by knots made too rapidly for me to follow, fastened the ends securely.

I had seen such motifs sewed here and there on
the tepees and had wondered if they had any particular significance. The only answer I got was
"*nacea*" ("perhaps"). But finally I was able to
learn of two of them, charms completely believed
in. One of these consisted of a bear's ear sewed to
a circlet further embellished by a beaded design.
A thong, sewed securely to this trinket, made possible its attachment to tepee or wearing apparel.
It was complete protection from all bears. Rattle-
snake rattles, used the same way, protected from
those snakes. I once owned a bear's-ear charm, and
it must have been potent, for the only encounter
I had with bears in all my experience was in cutting
bear steaks from the frozen fellow that hung in
my storehouse when I lived among the Cheyennes.
He had been given to me.

Mastincha's grown son was engaged in making
a pipe. His name was Sunka-hin-hota (Gray-
skinned dog), a name of which he was doubly
proud, since the gray dogs were held superior by
these Sioux. He had a narrow length—perhaps
two feet—of pipestone, as he called it. None of
this stone occurred in Dakota, he said, but had to

be obtained through trade with nomad tribes that
came from Minnesota. He had his little piece of
sharpened flint, and sat patiently grinding, grinding, at the opening in the stem of the pipe which
was already crudely fashioned. I learned that these
men sometimes worked for years at one pipe, for
it takes much time and patience to drill a canal in
a stem two feet long. When once the drilling has
been accomplished, the hard red stone is treated to
carving, painting, and polishing. The Sioux valued
his pipe next to his bow and war club. These men
vied with each other in contriving highly decorated
doeskin bags to hold pipe and kinnikinnick. Both
they and the Cheyennes made flutes, also, from
red stone. They were two-pipe flutes whose notes,
though minor and dolorous, were sweetly plaintive.

These Sioux were polygamous, a condition which
they considered exemplary, since it lessened child-
bearing and household labor for each squaw. If the
wives all liked each other they often lived together
in one great tepee, but, ordinarily, each wife preferred her own smaller dwelling. The provider for
several families had much hunting. Each squaw
had only her own and her children's clothing to
make, and but few duties to her husband.

The Sioux father taught his sons to ride. He tied
his little six-year-old to a pony and turned the
pony loose, to return home only when it chose to
or when he herded it back or lassoed it if it refused

to be herded. Stolidly and without struggling, the boy permitted himself to be tied fast, and just as stolidly would allow himself to be unbound, when he would run off in a matter-of-fact way into the tepee for food, or call a dog and run off to the prairies to play. The children, boys and girls, were always quiet and uncomplaining, and, apparently, fearless.

The boys were enormously proud of their scalp locks, which were never trimmed from birth to death. The hair upon a circular patch about the crown was braided just as soon as it became long enough. It was oiled at regular periods, and shown with much pride. I believe—though I have no certain proof—that it was never unbraided. The little boys mimicked their sires by running small goose or chicken feathers through these locks, but they were not permitted to use the eagle or hawk quills of their fathers.

Indian men and boys were never profane. The Sioux language has no oaths. The very worst that might be said, and it was never resorted to except under intense irritation, was, *"A hu ustan!"* ("I wish you would stop!") If the aggressor still persisted, the last resort was, *"Can te sica!"* ("Your heart is bad!") However, the men and women looked over the members of their own village groups, and often one heard, *"Nasula wanicha!"* ("No thinking with him—or her.") Or, as we

would say, "A brainless person." The double-play-
ing person was called two-tongued.

One of the last interviews I had at Oahi was
with an old man who looked at me with lusterless
eyes and answered what I asked of his Wankan-
Tanka—Great Spirit. The man's name was Gray
Hawk, and I had come to his tepee at his call, for
his little grandson had scalded his arm in the hot
soup. Even the old Indians knew by now that the
remedies I used were more certain and less painful
than those given them by their own medicine men.
After I had eased the little fellow's pain, I sat
down to talk with the grandfather who, alone and
desolate in the helplessness of old age, was happy
indeed to have me pay him all of my attention.
He was in a reciprocative mood, for I had just
helped his little child. He wanted to return the
favor.

"Tell me," I said, "about your Wankan-Tanka.
I do not know how big or brave he is nor where his
tepee stands."

"*Wankan-Tanka mahpie acta,*" ("The Great
Spirit has gone up into the heavens"), he said in
the tone of one explaining to a very young child.

"Then, if I cannot see him, tell me how he looks."

With that he told me, not by words so much as
by facial expression and the worshipful tones of
his deep old voice, that Wankan-Tanka, he of the
most brave heart, listens to and loves best those

who can suffer much pain and exert much courage
and strength; that he comes down to the tepee
where a brave lies dead and escorts him upon a
round of all the happy hunting grounds of heaven,
letting him choose and be completely satisfied with
the one among them all which he most desires. But
this journey of the two takes *wi wanji* (One month,
literally, one moon), so the body of the dead brave
must remain *wi wanji,* unentombed, and be fed
while the journey is in progress. I had seen the
bodies of the dead wrapped in blankets or furred
buffalo hides which were bound about them securely. They lay upon rude scaffolds fifteen to
twenty feet high. I had seen women coming in
the early gray of morning to replace the little bowls
of food with fresh grain. I had heard the wailing
and moaning at the feast of the dead. Now I asked
Gray Hawk about that.

"*Wi wanji, wi nampa, wi yamini, wi tepa, wi
zapan, wi shapi, wi shakoin, wi shadoin, wi napech-
ewaka, wi gemini, wi wanji, wi wampi,*" counted
the old chief in a sort of chant. *Wi* is moon; the
other words are Sioux for the numbers up to ten.
The last two repeat the first two. Thus, what he
said was, "After twelve moons, or, after a year." I
knew the feast of the dead followed long after
death.

He went on to describe the feast, its food, its
dance. Now must the people mourn, for, after

twelve months, the spirit has wandered too far to be followed in the happy hunting grounds. Men and women tortured themselves, the only way they knew to show the depth and sincerity of their grief. The men thrust sharp sticks through the calves of their legs and went out chanting their lament for the dead in a minor and monotonous tone. They took the path of most hazard of beast and weather, and it became a trail of blood, for they went on and on to the very limit of their endurance, often returning half frozen and insane with pain and fatigue. The women stayed in the tepees to tear their hair and mutilate their faces. The food of the feast was those articles the dead man had liked best when he lived, and was, in spite of grief, eaten with particular relish.

All this, Gray Hawk explained, was that the Great Spirit might have proof of men's power to suffer. Only through suffering, also, might men prove their love for the dead. Only through suffering might the living hope to please the all-brave, all-enduring Great Spirit. Gray Hawk here became very despondent, and fell into *hannedipi* (a god-seeking dream).

"And now," he said, "the Great Father at Washington has forbidden the Sun Dance!" How could the Great Spirit now know that the Sioux desired to please him?

I was unable to bring any comfort with my story

DAKOTA GHOST DANCE SONG
Edited by Thurlow Lieurance

Ya ha   i   hi   ya   ya ha   i   hi   ya   He ya   e   yo   e   yo   e—

e ———— e   Hi i yo   e   yo   He i yo   e   yo   Ee yo   i ya

he   yo   E yo   i ya   he ———— e ———— yo   Ateyapi   Xin   Ma - ka

o - wan - ca - ya   kawan   ni - si   pe - lo   he   ye   He - e ye   po   Ho

Oya   kapo   he ———— e   Oya   ka-pa   he ———— e ———— a ———— yo!

DAKOTA GHOST OR SPIRIT DANCE
(translation)

Lo, thus has the Father said, lo, thus he has commanded all
the world to sing, to sing. Thus has he said: Tell afar my
message: tell it afar!

Note—Short Bull, in 1888, in a vision of traveling to the
"spirit tipi," received a command to "teach the ghost dance
to all men." Through it men might "fall down as dead and
see the dead again." Thus was the Indian to proclaim love,
peace, clean speech, no murder, and brotherly help to all. Not
comprehending the portent of the "ghost dance," the militia
thought to end it by force. The massacre of several hundred
Indians at Wounded Knee resulted. The ghost dance is still
danced in other parts of the United States.

CHEYENNE SUN DANCE SONG

Edited by Thurlow Lieurance

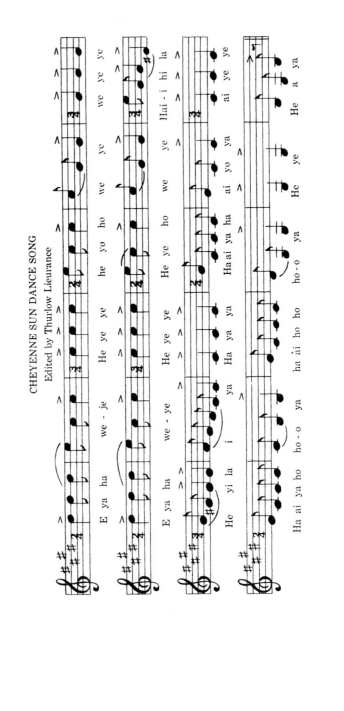

of my Great Spirit who asked only kindliness among all men together to be pleased.

A party had gone in midsummer to witness a Sun Dance somewhere near the site of the present Sisseton. I had accompanied them: I remembered all too well. We had arrived after the dance had begun. From a distance I could recognize the haphazard four-pole shelter which all these Indians erected hastily for feast or dance. It was roofed with branches and marsh-grass litter. Beneath this one was stored the unused paraphernalia of the dance. Beyond it, in the boiling sun, the dance was in full swing. Men clad in breechclouts only, moved in a maze of motion. They emitted a chant that died away and gathered volume with erratic irregularity.

At first I could not see for the haze of heat and the intervening heads of the Indian spectators who thronged about the place. The women stood or sat in groups and swayed back and forth, emitting an almost continuous moan with the same sort of religious fervor I afterwards witnessed in a congregation of Nazarenes. Somehow, for no apparent reason, I began to tremble from head to foot. I had stopped at some distance from the dancing place through an unworded dread of this Sun Dance. An inexplicable fear possessed me. I had seen Indians dancing before, and knew they had an endurance and swiftness of motion quite su-

perior to the white man's ability. What I was seeing seemed to be only a little more frenzied dance
than usual, with considerably more red paint
splotched on in unusual parts of the body. I moved
nearer to get a better view.

In horror I saw that the splotches were not red
paint, but blood—blood, spattering on the ground,
smearing the bodies of these maddened men. A
near-by dancer paused just long enough to lift the
skin of his breast and ram a sharpened stick, half
an inch thick, completely through, where he al-
lowed it to dangle painfully while he re-entered
the dance to whirl with redoubled speed. Arms,
legs, necks, breasts, were oozing blood from wooden
skewers. To shoulders, by wooden skewers, were
attached long deerskin ropes which trailed the
ground. Tied to these trailing ends were skeletons
of ox and buffalo heads which bounded after the
fleeing dancers, prodding their bleeding legs, and
by their weight tearing the flesh at the shoulders
where the thongs were attached.

One man dropped out, but shot up again and
went on. Desperately I shouted, "Oh, stop them!
Stop them! They are killing themselves! They
mustn't do it!"

"*Hna, hna, hna, taku waste!*" ("Well, well, well,
how very good!") came a slow cool voice beside me.

"Oh, but they will kill themselves!" I shrieked.

"No. They have strong heart, brave heart," she

answered with infinite pride. "Mine has a very brave heart."

Here one of the dancers fell and did not rise. He lay there inert for some minutes, when the crowd parted and with praiseful and congratulatory grunts saluted the old squaw who made her way to the prostrate man, lifted him, and bore him away from the dancing area. I could see no more. With hands over my eyes I stumbled out to where we had lariated our ponies, mounted, and rode furiously away, in what direction I neither knew nor cared. I rode until I could no longer hear the weird chant, then drew rein, leaped from my pony, and, hiding my face in the hot grass, wept fiercely.

Now, when old Gray Hawk said, "How will the Great Spirit know that the Sioux are men who can suffer?" this Sun Dance in the midst of stifling August afternoon heat rose again before me. I said some futile words and went away, leaving old Gray Hawk looking after me with sad, lusterless eyes.

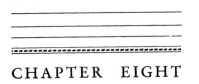

CHAPTER EIGHT

Now, after two years, I had earned a vacation. I sped back to Washington to spend a few weeks. My wonder at the uselessness of women at home was only redoubled, so, when the letter came appointing me to a new Indian center among the Cheyennes, in the Cheyenne River Reservation, I left for Valentine, Nebraska, with even more enthusiasm than I had gone to Springfield.

Old Kate did not weep over me this time. Instead, she looked upon me with revering awe, and bragged about me constantly. Mother, too, seemed somewhat less sure of her reasons for leading the social life. Father was so proud of me he was simply ridiculous. I was feted and entertained and taken the rounds in Washington, and Father and I stole off for a week together at Deer Park in the Allegheny Mountains west of Washington.

The train across Nebraska was slow and dirty, and I was willing to change to the stage which was to meet the train at Valentine, long before the little one-coach, grimy train drew into the station. To my surprise the platform was crowded with

cowboys and Indians, gay with embroidered boots,
chaps, silk handkerchiefs, feathers, and paint. As
I rose to alight I saw through the smoky window
that they were swarming to the coach entrance.
Since I was the only passenger, I hesitated. The
conductor drew me down the aisle after him, saying, "Better get down on this other side."

He handed me into the arms of a stalwart cowboy in white chaps and a sombrero, shining boots,
and spurs. The fellow bowed with his hand over
his heart and offered me an elbow. As I reached
to take it, thinking he had been sent to meet me,
he fired a pistol above my head. At this signal the
mob swirled about the end of the coach, pistols
popping, war whoops ringing. I was too frightened
to move, and stood limply in the midst of the hubbub until the stage came dashing up. The driver
saw my predicament and rushed the crowd with
his long whip. He got me and my baggage safely
aboard the stagecoach. There were seven other passengers—all rough-looking men—but I sat back
gratefully among them, wondering at the ease of
my delivery and not understanding the situation
at all, until the driver said, "Now don't y' be gettin'
scared, Miss. They's jist givin' the new teacher a
little celebration." I have often seen modern children playing the game they call "Cowboy and Indian," and they get the spirit of the thing.

All of that night and most of the next day the

stage crawled on over one rough butte after the
other. At first we passengers were too well packed
to jounce much. The warmed footstones taken
aboard at Valentine grew cold, the wind howled
and swayed the coach until it seemed it must upset.
The country grew wilder, and, at last, even the
trail ahead disappeared. Towards evening, after
all the other passengers had disembarked, we stopped to change horses. After that I saw not even
so much as a tepee or trading post. It had been
raining since sunrise, and the horses, even the fresh
ones, tugged and sweated to move at a walk
through the mud. Near dark the driver halted and
jumped down to open the stage door with, "Your
stop, Miss."

I dismounted and looked about. Below me swept
the turbulent Cheyenne River. On the hill slope
above I could just make out in the fading light a
low, rambling log house with one tree before the
door. A fat old Indian squaw appeared, ambling
slowly down the hill.

She proved to have many chins and merry eyes.
She welcomed me with all the warmth of a fond
mother. She felt my slender arms and legs, not
once, but over and over, and shook her head profoundly each time. I thought she might be sixty-
five.

Arrived at her cabin, she set about at once to
make me comfortable, moving with surprising

briskness at her tasks of replenishing the fire, heating the *wasena,* bringing in extra blankets. I found
in the first half-hour that she was a scorner of men.
No, indeed, she was *not* married!

An old-maid Indian? I wondered, and went
on to draw her story from her. She was not in the
least reticent, but answered everything with the
utmost frankness, and even interpolated some not
too complimentary comments on the value of the
male. She was as pleased with my name as I was
surprised at hers. It was Elizabeth.

On her own initiative she had gone down to the
Government agency and had stayed long enough
to learn something of a white man's house and its
keeping, of his beliefs and religion. The name
"Elizabeth" had seemed to her the best white man's
name for a woman that she had been able to learn,
so Elizabeth she became.

Her house was a large low room made of logs
and chinked inside and out with mud. A second
little storage room, unconnected with the big room,
was woven of willows. The house sat high up the
steep bank of the Cheyenne River with a winding
path down to the water's edge. Elizabeth's Government stove was placed in the center of the room,
Indian fashion. One corner of the room was graced
by a great box holding Elizabeth's personal possessions. A second box in a second corner held cooking
utensils. The third corner held Elizabeth's rude

hewn bed, the fourth a deal table upon which sat
a kerosene lamp. Intervening spaces along the
walls were occupied by rude backless benches.

She was jovial, indeed. Her double chins often
shook with mirth, for she was apparently happy
to be free and unmarried. When an Indian woman
of forty winters has had no suitors, she is ostracized
from regular society. From what she said, Elizabeth must always have been fat and double-chinned,
thereby forfeiting any claim to lovers. How she
laughed about that! With what I took to be a
twinkle in her eye—although her words did not bear
it out—she told me that all the Indians, men and
women alike, were hers to govern, and that they
stood in awe of her. When she called them to her
house they came and listened to her as long as she
cared to talk. Singlehanded, and against tradition as
old as her race, Elizabeth, an old-maid Sioux Indian,
was bossing a camp. She had decided she would have
neither gambling nor stealing. She ended this as-
tounding speech by saying that she had learned of
me and my courage at the agency and had sent for
me to help her accomplish this thing. Did I not have
the wisdom she lacked? Did she not have the strong
body I did not have? The two, together, could do
it! Was it all, I wonder, her way of getting even
for her spinsterhood?

Tradition made Elizabeth live apart from her
family, but the same tradition provided her with

food, since a portion of family supplies must be set aside for the one dishonored through being unwed, although she might not eat it in the presence of her family. Tradition also dictated that such a woman must provide her own blankets, wood, and water. All this I learned within the first hour. She rejoiced openly at my every word, and was so solicitous for the comfort of my slight person that I unbent completely and called her *"Ina"* ("Mother") that first night. It pleased her mightily and sealed an enduring friendship.

I didn't care much for coddling, though, and being treated like a doll that would break. I insisted upon doing my share of the work. Ina was astonished into silence by my strength and endurance. All she could do was to groan enthusiastically over me. Thus, from the first, I went to the river for water. Ina would haul two ten-gallon jars by a twin move and hoist them to her shoulders. I could manage one that held perhaps three gallons. She would stride ahead, bareheaded, out into the chill air, bound to her pony's back, and lead the way down the angled path. The river was frozen along the bank, but the swift-running current in the center was uncoated. She waded out, or walked out, as need happened, and filled the jars. I did not follow. Shifting about skillfully with her feet, she filled the jars without herself sinking into the quicksand. We walked the ponies up the hill so as not to spill any water. Once, as we were making our difficult way up the bank, I suddenly wondered what Marian and Mother would say could they see me now, bareheaded, bareback and astride a lean pony, swathed in an Indian blanket, balancing my jar of water on my shoulder and trailing cheerfully behind fat old Ina, astride, also, and balancing her two great jars on either hip. She always looked me over skeptically when we reached the house. Invariably, when she found me unbroken, she would put her hands on her hips and laugh so hard that I was obliged to join her.

She was enormously delighted with my clothing and trinkets. I often caught her eyeing me as one might a pile of gold. Every night she went out to the storeroom, brought in my blankets and skins, put two of the backless benches together and smoothed and patted until I had a comfortable bed, much, much more smoothing than she gave her own. The softest blankets were placed next to me. My bed was nearest the fire.

Elizabeth had stored a prodigious amount of wood in the room; it all but filled it. Outside temperatures of forty below soon ate into it, and I found myself one gray afternoon trailing Ina down to the timber for wood. The sky seemed low enough to touch, and there was a fall of fine, cutting snow. She carried no tools but a strong old blanket and a tomahawk. Ina gathered the heavier branches that had been brought down by wind or age, and I the lighter ones. We piled them on the blanket until we had collected about as much as a pony might pull. Ina got to her knees, tied one end of the blanket about her ample waist, and asked me to give her the two remaining corners of the blanket. By tugging my best I was finally able to pull the two free corners to within Ina's grasp. Bending her head backward, she brought the corners in front of her face, tied them into a knot, and took the knot between her teeth. With a single mighty effort she got to her feet. It was my turn to stare as she hoisted her load. She swayed dreadfully for just a second, then took up her talk and the homeward journey in such a wholly matter-of-fact way that it made me feel as small and useless as the smallest, driest twig in Ina's pack.

It was good to be indoors that night, for the wind rose and the snow fell faster and faster. By midnight a blizzard was raging. In the morning the tree before the door was invisible. Ina and I were cut off from everything. I had never witnessed more genuine pleasure and pride than that with which Ina took down the blankets and bags that hung about on the rafters and from their contents cooked steaming and hearty, if strange-flavored, foods that cheered her foster child. She served squaw corn, shelled from little purple, red, yellow, and white speckled ears braided together by their husks and festooned from the ceiling. She crushed the grains in her mortar and boiled the meal all day. She cooked dried beans and dried turnips. I wondered how the little field mice who had hoarded the beans were faring. It did not occur to me to feel disgust at eating what a mouse had once carried in its mouth. The Cheyenne River was as clear as glass, and the beans were cooked all day. We had berries, too, cooked from her dried store. She went about, wholly unperturbed by the violent storm which terrorized me. She worked incessantly at her cooking, fire tending, beading.

How we talked! Really talked, there in that rude cabin, shut away from the rest of the world. She asked and answered, and I asked and answered until that day with its closeness of spiritual touch became a high light of my whole life. People rarely talk, have real communication. I made much progress in the Cheyenne tongue, too, that day, for Ina knew only "meat, sugar, flour, soap, beans," in English—necessary words at the agency store—and would make no effort to learn more.

Of course this, my first blizzard, passed, it and many another one, until the weather began to moderate and visitors began to drift in. There were no tepees in sight of our house, but they were close, Ina said. A great many young men came. That visibly disturbed Ina. They appraised me as a little girl might look at her first doll. All of them were against the Government school because it ruled out scalp locks and painted faces. Would I teach them as they were, pig-tailed and painted?

One night three of them called together. *Would I teach them?* They sat, smoking their kinnikinnick leisurely, waiting an answer. I soon saw they would wait until I did answer, however long that might be. So I agreed to do it and to loan them pencils and slates. It was decided that they should come every night. I said, though, that I did not want to teach boys with painted faces. Paint was ugly to me. With scornful grunts, a little tinged with disappointed surprise, they at last agreed to come unpainted. Shortly after, I heard their moccasins crunching on the hardened snow outside. I looked out the door after them, black figures, blanketed closely, moving silently across a brilliant white expanse of starlit snow—Dog Bear, Gray Bear, and White Owl.

These three came regularly and were soon joined by others, so that in a short time I had a class of fifteen. They were serious, industrious, and naïvely pleased with each new accomplishment. It was a delight to teach them, and I looked forward to their coming. Every evening, when the low winter sun set, Ina would build up a roaring fire while I set my lighted lamp and books in readiness. It was cozy inside, though palpitatingly cold without, a cold cruel to walk in. Yet they always came, blank-

eted heavily. Stopping just a moment about the
fire, they came over to the table eager to work. The
three R's, a little geography, and music filled the
evening. They liked writing and soon became good
penmen.

After several weeks had passed, and the air, even
though the snow was still deep, began to have the
faintest feel of spring, a new boy came one night.
His white blanket was the most beautiful I had
yet seen, and I stared at it because I could not help
it. It was a pure gleaming white doeskin, entirely
unornamented. He gave no response to anything
I said to him. Somewhat irritated, I went about the
usual program until we came to singing. I asked
him to join us. He remained mute. Quite angry, I
turned to the others and asked who this stranger
with such rude ways might be. The faintest flicker
of amusement crossed their faces, and all they
would say was their exasperating *nacea* (perhaps).

Old Ina lay snoring in her bed as she usually did
during classes. She was no longer young and she
worked hard all day. Nothing in the social customs
of these Indians decried her sleeping thus. That she
was my adopted mother, that I stayed in the house
with her after sunset—these things fulfilled all
their law. Tonight she was snoring uncommonly
loud, for she was unusually fatigued, having walked
miles through the snow to attend the birth of a
papoose in one of the farthest tepees.

We wakened her with our lusty singing. She rubbed her eyes, yawned, and sat up. I saw her face take on a look of antagonism as she saw the stranger wrapped in his white blanket before the fire. After the singing the boys stayed on to ask questions, and in the midst of it Ina dozed off again. When the boys at last left, White Blanket left with them. He had not so much as told me his name. I looked from the door after them as they descended the hill, singing together the song we had sung last. The snow was deep and crusted, and they walked over the great drifts with little noise. I missed White Blanket. He must live in another direction, I thought.

Ina still snored. She had always gone out at night to bring in my bedding, but tonight, I thought as I looked at her tired old face, I would not disturb her, but would get it myself, although she had always cautioned me particularly never, never, to do so. I opened the door quickly and ran around the house to the storeroom.

As I reached the second corner I was seized by strong arms, wrapped tightly in a white doeskin blanket, and borne swiftly away by noiseless feet—all in an instant, it seemed to me. The blanket bound me so tightly I could not call out. I could not move so much as a little toe. Swiftly, noiselessly, I was borne down the path towards the river, on, on. I do not know how far I had been carried when, through the blanket, I thought I heard a sound such as Ina might make if she were terribly angry. Nearer and more distinct it grew until, when it seemed right at hand, with one incredible move of my captor I was unblanketed and deposited in the deepest part of a very deep snowdrift. Certainly I saw neither man nor blanket, nor could I tell in what direction he had disappeared.

Up floundered old Ina, puffing like a donkey engine and scolding violently and most illogically, *"Taku shica achen?"* ("What bad thing is this?") *"Cea sni!"* ("Don't cry!") "This is foolish, foolish! How silly white women are!"

I might have been an Egyptian mummy for all the power to move I had. Without the least help from me she pulled me from the drift, scolding vigorously all the time, wrapped me in half her blanket. It was not the one she usually wore, but her largest and finest, I noticed from my paralyzed daze. On stumbling feet she half dragged, half carried me back over the trail along which I had been so precipitously borne. I collapsed when she got me back to the fire and dumped me on a bench. I could still hear, but no longer understand her scolding words. When she saw my state she had the decency to quiet her voice, but she kept on interminably. When I came to she was mumbling a kind of incantation, which grew in fervency as she saw I was more and more conscious of things. A nauseating mixture was bubling on the stove.

Now she began rubbing my disrobed body with the slimy stuff, a thick greenish brown soup. I made a faint objection. She rubbed more briskly. Fiercely she muttered between her teeth, over and over, that Blue Star would never be carried off again.

The heat, the nasty odor, and my natural hardihood combined to revive me completely, but I was powerless before Ina's unasked and unwanted ministrations, which went on for close to two hours, when she finally desisted. Dimly I began to see some connection between the bizarre events of this night. I ventured to ask Ina a question or two. From her sputtering and scolding I finally knew the truth. The white blanket is worn by the Cheyenne man who seeks a mate. I had spoken to him; therefore I approved of him. I had left my house—alone, and after sunset—final proof of my approval and interest, and he had been in his own right to attempt to carry me off. I retraced his trail the next day. He had carried me to within possibly two hundred feet of his tepee. Had he once entered it with me, by the law of the Cheyennes I would have been his lawful squaw and property from that hour forward. Now I understood Ina's wild scolding. Now I remembered with what seriousness she had warned me to stay inside the house after sunset. I understood it all, now—except the smelly soup with which I reeked.

After much incoherent speech because of her

still flaming anger, I learned the side-splitting truth: Ina had subjected me to the Cheyenne charm against suitors! She, thinking in the marriage customs of her people, could scarcely be convinced that I had not been a willing captive. Had I not given a man wearing a white blanket every positive signal?

It was long after midnight before I was able to convince her that I was horrified by the episode, and that my immobility had been from terror, not stubbornness. I did not try to walk back to the hut because I couldn't. I was too scared. I went over it in every way I could. Finally, I told her of our marriage customs. When she found out the truth, she set down the jar in which she was still violently stirring some of her herb charm against suitors, and laughed until her sides and double chins danced.

I was still trembling. Ina became all solicitation. My bed was brought in, smoothed, and warmed. I was led to it like an invalid and covered with great tenderness. I knew that the adult Indian never kissed. Impulsively, I threw my arms about Ina's neck and kissed her. She stood back, arms akimbo, and eyed me with a strange new emotion twisting her old face. Then Ina bent and kissed me. She had saved me from the very horror which now I saw my father might have known of. Weak and unstrung, I lay snugly between the blankets Ina tucked about me, and cried and cried.

I could not sleep. I relived the experience over and over. Now I knew why the youth had such a fine necklace of carved deer toes, why his moccasins were beaded all over, even on the soles, and had little beaded trailers. I finally dozed a little, but Ina's angry voice would wake me. I could hear her yelling savagely, *"Taki da he ye Wichipitowan, Wichipitowan! Taku wilakaiakata! Ayu stan yu!"* ("Blue Star, Blue Star, where are you going? How foolish! Now you stop!")

The next day I learned that my suitor was Matela, a man who already had several wives. Since I had had such a narrow escape, I decided to ask Ina all about the marriage customs of her people, that I might act more intelligently in the future. I looked ruefully at my besmeared face in my little hand mirror. Almost angrily I turned to Ina.

"Will this stay on?"

Ina laughed and pointed to the water jar. I set water to heating on the stove, and while it heated I drew from Ina a complete recital of the courtship and marriage customs of the Cheyennes.

Again and again I had seen a certain quick, intense, and meaningful look exchanged by boys and girls. The Indian word for this look, if literally translated, would be "eye-set." But the young people were never permitted to walk together. The girls always stayed with their mother or a group of women. They must not go out unaccompanied after sunset. They were painfully shy and easily embarrassed and hid their faces in their blankets at the least pretext. As soon as a girl had decided which of the youths she preferred and had sent him her message with her bright eyes, she must at once make known the fact to the other girls of the camp —a sort of "taken" label, so that no other girl might consider him. Only after the message had been flashed might the youth inquire—of others—her name, her father's rank and wealth. This information was necessary, for he must decide if he be able to pay the price her rank and wealth demanded before he might aspire to marry her. If he could pay, he might then begin his wooing. Far out among the hills yet still in sight of her tepee, he now must go to play his two-pipe red-stone flute. I had heard these flutes and known that lovers played them, but had supposed the girls to be close by.

If the girl approved her musician she might show her pleasure by standing motionless outside the door of her tepee until the music ended, often an hour or more. Displeasure was signified by a prompt return indoors. Should the lovers disobey convention and attempt a rendezvous, woe to the girl! She must endure the ignominy of yielding to the charm against suitors that I had had to endure at Ina's hands. Thereafter she usually waited a long time before she became of interest to another youth. If a woman reached the age of forty without having sent a preference telegram, she was doomed to live alone and provide her own blankets and fuel and water.

I was but twenty-two. After this talk with Ina, whenever I heard a flute in the hills or across the level grasslands after dusk along the Cheyenne River, I took a strange new delight in knowing that beside some tepee leaned a shy young girl trying to read her own desires and the mystery of love.

No Indian girl would make an out-and-out declaration of her love to another woman. She would handle the matter something like this, nonchalantly, to a companion: "Do you know that Sleeping Bear is splendid? Well, look at that tall, powerful man over there. That is he. Has he not a good heart?"

When, after much flute playing in the dusk, the wooer had won his maid, hers was the next responsibility. She must obtain the chief's permission to go out and join her lover. I had a chance one summer to witness the ceremony attending the granting of such a request. It is one of the scenes that is indelibly painted in my memory with all the fresh vividness of yesterday.

CHAPTER NINE

A GREAT shelter had been erected upon the open prairie. It was built of cottonwood saplings and thatched with coarse branches and marsh grass. Here a hundred Indians, perhaps, had gathered, when I rode up on my pony. In their midst stood the chief, arms folded. I dismounted to wait with the rest. After a time the crowd parted, and down the aisle they thus made came a girl, alone. She was gorgeously dressed in orange calico and a brilliantly beaded blanket. Her long black hair streamed unbound about her. Her face was checkered with red and yellow paint. I heard the women near me whispering that her father had asked a white pony, two eagle feathers, and five blankets for her. She came on slowly and with beautiful dignity stopped before the chief, her head bowed. The chief removed her blanket.

I was not near enough to hear the one sentence she spoke, but it was a question. Nor could I understand the chief's response. Later I learned that one was not expected to. His tone and gesture told plainly of an affirmative answer. The long speech which followed seemed to be advice.

DAKOTA LOVE SONG

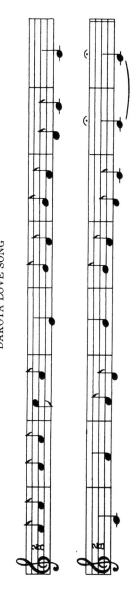

Cheyenne Youth

Then, from the outskirts of the gathering, came the youth, gaudy with paint, brave in brilliant feather and blanket. He strode up to the chief with swaggering gait to the jangle of deer-toe bracelets and necklaces. He laid his hand in the chief's hand, and the chief took the girl's hand and laid it within the youth's. After another brief and half-audible speech the chief returned the blanket to the girl's shoulders. Both she and her lover returned by separate routes through the crowd to rejoin their own families. This was not the real wedding. Now that she had the chief's consent, that night the girl would go out to meet her piping sweetheart and he would carry her to his tepee.

The next day the camp was bustling with preparation of the marriage feast. Under the shelter the women spread down their finest painted deerskins. Upon these they placed baskets of wild plums, both fresh and dried, and smaller vessels of Juneberries. The largest earthern jars were filled with steaming meat and turnip stew. In the center, the crowning glory of the feast stood the huge bowl of *wasena,* the paste made of wild cherries, marrow, and lean meat, a kind of mincemeat. Today the little dried cakes in which it was stored had been cooked in much liquid to make a kind of relish.

The prairie lay level here, but rippled away to meet circling hills. How vividly I remember how the scene glowed in the light of the setting sun, a gaudy, yet lovely picture. Brilliant color of blanket, feather, jar, odor of savory food, the wedding guests coming in on pony or travois, the whispered gossip among the women that the groom was receiving more gifts than he had paid for his bride—all combined to make an unforgettable memory.

I ate with the rest—good food, as I recall it. But the revelry grew more and more spirited. I stole to my pony and rode away at a walk across the short buffalo grass. I do not know how long the celebration lasted, but I heard tom-toms and shouting far into the night, for I could not sleep. Next day the shelter had disappeared, and nothing was left to show that once again, marriage, that mystery and necessity of the race, had been consummated yesterday there on the prairie.

It was seventy-five miles to the Cheyenne Agency. The journey had to be made in one of the Government-issued wagons which would contain many times what could be dragged in a *toksu* (travois). Ordinarily these wagons stood about unused, and the men often gambled them tongueless and wheelless. Wagon bed and running gears were held in disdain except for the infrequent trips to the agency. Then the wagons were reassembled.

I had not left Elizabeth's camp since my arrival, nor had I seen another white person. I was the only white person between Elizabeth's camp and the agency. The snow had all melted, when an old In-

dian woman asked me to accompany her on a trip
to the agency. I was as eager to go as if she had
asked me to go to Europe. Though the countryside
was green it was still uncomfortably cold sitting on
the high wagon seat. The team was an excitable
span of half-broken beasts, and we jolted and lunged
over the trail at a crawl, for the ground was soaked
with melted snow and the gumbo would collect
about the heavy wooden wheel spokes until we
would come to a standstill. My companion had been
over this trail before. She would vault over the
wheel, taking with her a wooden paddle she had
brought along for the purpose, and jam and scrape
and cudgel the wheels free of mud. On our first
stop I took the chance to slip down into the wagon
bed, where I made myself warm and comfortable
on the blankets there. The trail was long and laborious and we were to camp along the way, so we had
blankets, cooking pots, and tepee.

The sticky mud collected again and again, and
the stoical driver jumped down to jam it off. The
earth grew wetter, our stops more frequent, and I
decided to help at mud jamming. I had to get out
so often that I finally left the endgate of the wagon
to dangle. Whether it was the noise of the endgate
banging, or the sudden new lightness of the wheels,
or the sharp cut of the whip, I don't know, but
after one of our stops I was ignominiously seated in
the middle of the muddy road by a sudden rearing

and running of the team. I was thrown right into
the midst of the sloshy trail, while the wagon raced
away farther and farther. My best yelling elicited
no response. I got up and tried to run. The more
effort I made, the farther away the wagon appeared
to be. It was worse than any nightmare, for when
one dreams he is pumping his legs valiantly and
can't gain any distance, that is fearful enough, but
here I was heaving like a plow horse and going back-
wards! I slipped and slid in the treacherous mud,
but kept the wagon in sight. Pictures of wolf packs
killing cattle, of wandering Indian braves stealing
squaws, of bears, coyotes, all and more of the perils
conjured up by Mother in Washington, beset me
here in broad daylight, and I got ahead somehow,
impelled not so much by muscle as by fear. For
the first time since I had entered Dakota I quaked
with apprehension.

I looked up to find that I had gained on the
wagon. It was stopping! Of course! The wheels
were mudded again. As I came up the "squaw who
never laughed" was howling with laughter. Tears
spattered her mud paddle. Miles farther on she
broke out in a chuckling exclamation: "A white
woman run as fast as Indian!"

After two weary days we drove into the agency.
My grim companion seemed in fine trim, but I was
stiff and weary. I had slept for the first time in a
drafty and smoky tepee. My right shoulder was

useless from mud jamming, for I had held up my end of that labor all the way in, the entire seventy-five miles. Fifty years later I visited the "squaw who never laughs" in a little hut by the highway. She was making moccasins to sell to tourists. She still had a little picture I had given her, which she exhibited with great pride. Then she laughed—the querulous, high-pitched laugh of those who are very old—remembering my run in the mud. "A white woman run as fast as Indian," she cackled, slapping her bony knee.

It was this same woman who told me of the Cheyenne baby lore. When the baby is born it is oiled very thoroughly and laid within the leather carrier with its arms and legs straightened and bound tightly against the tough and unyielding backpiece which is often made of hardwood. This carrier is lined with soft buffalo hair and folds snugly about the child, holding its body rigidly against the backpiece. For one month the child remains thus, encased like a worm in its chrysalis. It is never removed from it, but is fed and tended by means of flaps about the case which may be opened. Indians believe that the curved arms and legs of the newborn must be straightened at once, and certainly a month-old baby is nearly as straight as its sire. The leather cradle is hung within the tepee or out of doors upon a tree if the weather is not too cold, for ample protection is afforded by the many layers of soft leather. In spite of their fine inheritance, Indian babies died in largest numbers in this first month of existence. Many died, too, when they were graduated from the cradle to the blanket and rode about on their mothers' backs.

After the first month the baby rides pack-a-back. The Indian mother is expert in anchoring her burden by firm and efficient knots of her shoulder blanket. She may tie the end of the carrying blanket about her forehead, or under her chin, or even carry it between her teeth. The lower edge of the blanket is tied securely about the mother's waist in such a way that the baby's feet have no chance to move. A baby sometimes rides on its mother's back until it is three or four years old. To place the child, the mother takes it by its arms and flings it over her shoulder to her back, where it clings to her neck with its hands until she has secured the blanket knots. Indian babies never have colic, for their stomachs are always warm, but, since the mother must go about her manual labor, the baby's back is subjected to the rigors of outdoor cold, and many die of pneumonia. I have seen Indian mothers kissing their tiny babies. At least they touched their lips to the cheek of the blinking little red fellow and chanted their soothing *"Chinca chestina, chinca, Chestina,"* a little melody of lullaby running like this:

CHEYENNE LULLABY MOTIF

Ma - chin - cha mit - a-wa

They sing it over and over, changing key, up and down the scale, so that the song can be made to go on indefinitely. I learned to sing it, and often tried my skill with the younger children when they were tired. Later, I sang it to my own children. The Indian women always sang in a low tone and never carried the highest note above three-space treble "C." It was sung with closed lips.

The Cheyennes or Sioux never punished their children and never were impatient with disobedience. A mother might call a child to help, and the child might play half the morning before obeying. It was always approved when it did come, never chided. Children played incessantly in the daytime but listened quietly to tales and instruction told them about the fire in the evening.

Early in the spring the Indian agent wrote me that I was to go by the next stage to another center, where he said I would meet the "uncivilized Indian."

CHAPTER TEN

Nᴇᴡ ᴀɴᴅ exciting experiences fairly hustled each other from the scene, they came so fast. My new home bore the vivid name of Cut Meat Creek. For a long time, it seemed, this creek had been the gathering place of Indian women who came from great distances at stated seasons to prepare the winter store of meat. The camp was buzzing with women's voices when I arrived.

I walked out among them, somewhat dazed. They gabbled like geese and merely endured my presence, making no effort to return any kind of answers to my remarks. As long as I could not talk to them, I thought, perhaps I can learn something from watching. I stood about, and at last followed the crowd down to the edge of the creek. Here, forked cottonwood saplings had been set in the ground, fork up. Across every two such forked saplings a transverse pole lay. Now the women began their show.

I have seen sleight-of-hand performances and exhibits of skill with knives, but these Indian women could have made a fortune now-a-days exhibiting what to them was an everyday accomplishment. With one hand they lifted a quarter of some animal carcass from the piles of freshly killed animals that lay all about. With incredible endurance and steady muscle they held the thing aloft with the left hand while with the right they sliced the flesh into long strips, cut almost as evenly as if by a modern slicing machine. The scene was both odorous and bloody, but the women seemed to relish it immensely as they walked back and forth to hang their sliced meat upon the racks made of cottonwood saplings. They stood upon big jars to reach the racks, and hung up their meat, some strips two feet long. There was an enormous pile to cut up and dry, and since there seemed to be no further operation, I left the scene in some haste. I was squeamish, I knew, for I ate this same kind of bloody meat myself—people everywhere did—but I had never before seen such a lot of blood and sharp knives at one time. The evident enjoyment of these Indian women made me see this human attribute we call appetite in a new aspect. I wondered long upon the way this life of ours is sustained by the lives of our humbler brothers.

But the meat cutting was completely transcended by the event which next took place. Would I go to their dance? they asked, and rejoiced openly when I said I would. It was well for me that I did not know what I was accepting. The dance was yet

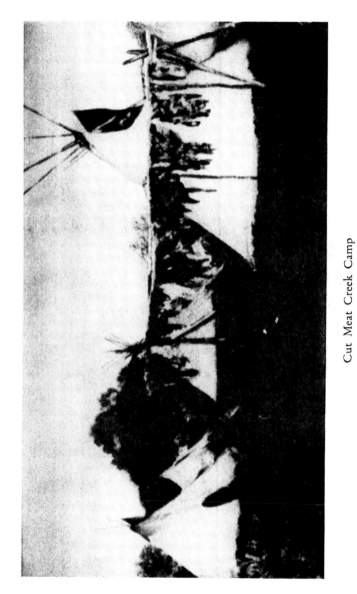

Cut Meat Creek Camp

Coming into Camp

one moon distant, but preparation for it went on feverishly, day after day. English society makes extensive preparations for its functions, but this preparation could have been paralleled only by a British coronation. There was not the littlest acorn jangling with its fellows from its leathern thong that did not get a magnificent polishing. There was talk of nothing but the dance. A little at a time I learned that this dance was an annual occasion, when the Teton Sioux entertained their neighbors, the Crows. I had learned the Sioux speech from Mr. Riggs at the school near Springfield. His father had compiled a Sioux-English dictionary. But these Cut Meat Creek Sioux spoke Teton Sioux, which differed quite decidedly from the pronunciation and vocabulary I had learned. I did my best and listened hard, but I was oftener than not met with a disgusted "Good not!" when I tried to talk with these Indians. I lent a hand at the work where I could, imitated their speech, and finally won their favor.

Never have I witnessed such unflagging industry. The Indian man is deliberate in everything he does, and leaves the hurrying for the women. He works in a leisurely way, rests often, delegates all things which must be done regularly to his long-suffering squaw. But now he became another fellow. He helped to make new clothing for everybody, including the children. Shirts and moccasins, beaded and adorned with porcupine quills, flowed into the common warehouse. The men made new war bonnets and furbished up old. They caught, broke, and groomed wild range ponies, which they would give as presents. They made the dance floor.

There was an enormous log shelter in this camp, evidently of recent construction. It was dedicated to dancing. The men brought pots of boiling water and poured it carefully and evenly over the dirt floor. When the water had soaked in, they pounded the floor with clubs. Hour after hour they pounded. A second pouring of water followed, and a second pouring. They worked at it for days with boiling water and clubs until they considered it satisfactory. It was surprisingly smooth and even. As far as I saw, they used no level of any kind.

As the day approached, all work was speeded, and the women ran about feverishly, for, besides preparing enormous quantities of food, they must now also assist in the painting of their husband's bodies. They took infinite care in this and did it with the utmost pride. The finished braves were hideous to my eyes, for their entire bodies were done in grotesque designs in orange, blue, green, purple, and red, all startlingly brilliant. The Indian wife is valued first for her skill as a body painter. Cooking is secondary.

The cooking was a long and laborious job, for the women brought all of the wood and carried all of the water and did all of the lifting of the heavy pots, in addition to the actual fire tending and food preparation. They prepared the same things I had eaten at the wedding feast, *wasena*, meat stew with vegetables, and variously prepared fruits. In addition they made bushel after bushel of "Dakota bread." Corn was first ground in hollowed stone mortars and a dough made of it by adding water and melted fat. This mixture was blended by pounding, and was finally moulded into long black ropes. Half-inch slices, scored several times on the flat side, were tossed into boiling fat and fried brown, and they came from the fragrant fat as brown and almost as tempting as doughnuts.

At last the day arrived, and the guests began to swarm in. Over the hills they came with toksu-loads of babies, household utensils, presents, and tepees, or on ponies. A few came in shiny new Government wagons. Everyone was trigged out in what were apparently new holiday garments made recently for this occasion. In they flocked, laughing, talking, laden with gifts. In a few minutes after each arrival the women had strung together their three tepee poles, set them up, rammed in the remaining poles, and spread the highly ornamented skin cover in place where it was secured by double "buttonholes" and small sharpened sticks. Fires sent up smoke, and children played completely at home before their own tepee doors. Dogs were everywhere, barking and racing with children. By noon a good-sized town of tepees nestled in the ravine that had been tenantless—except for a rabbit or two—at sunrise. The color, the high spirits, the activity, made the scene unforgettable. Surely, I thought, here is the Indian at his best.

At sundown the children were put to bed. No crying was heard, then or later, and they must have slept soundly through the loudest, wildest, and most continuous bedlam I had yet heard.

With great bravado two other white guests and I were led into the dance shelter and seated together. At the opposite end from us sat the squaws, beating the tom-toms which we had been hearing long before we entered. All the braves were lined up along one side, some also beating tom-toms. These players now broke out in an excited rhythm, and the women took the floor.

Their dance was a strange and mystic weaving in and out, done occasionally to offset the regular measure of the dance, which was done without moving the feet. Standing in irregular columns, the women twisted, turned, and shook their bodies to the monotonous tom-toms. It became very humdrum to watch—the same thing over and over. They did not resume their seats for nearly an hour.

Then up sprang the braves into a dance that was madness itself. Slowly at first, but gathering momentum and intensity, they danced on interminably, yelling, shaking brilliant rattles and tomahawks. They worked themselves into a near frenzy which of itself was frightening to behold. But my heart stood still when I heard my own name called, over and over.

"Wichipitowan, Wichipitowan, Wichipitowan, inajan we!" ("Blue Star, Blue Star, Blue Star, rise up!")

Trembling violently, I permitted myself to be drawn into the very vortex of this mass of yelling, whirling, naked men. They wore only the breech-clouts, to which some had attached lengths of brilliant cloth which trailed after them like demon's tails. Round and round me they spun, waving their hatchets with upward sweeps right against my face, daubing my cheeks with paint; closer, farther, in and out, until I was dizzy with fear and the frantic motion before my eyes. Faster and faster they whirled; louder and louder they whooped; and I was half blinded by a great splash of paint thrown into my face just as someone seized me and whirled me dizzily. When I could have dropped from exhaustion the dancing stopped suddenly, the whooping ceased, and I felt a blanket thrown about me, a gorgeous blanket, the labor of many months.

The whole assembly remained motionless and absolutely quiet. The Teton chief arose.

"There has come among us," he said, "a most wise woman, Blue Star, who teaches wisdom to our

children in our tepees and brings many gifts of
wisdom to our people."

Here he strode grandly up to me and presented
me with an eagle feather.

"Blue Star is of the brave heart," he went on,
and heaped praise upon me, not omitting the detail
—which had traveled even to this place—that I
had hit a fleeing rabbit with an arrow. The crowd
parted to admit a youth who led a beautiful white
pony, which was also presented to me. Others
came up with moccasins and trinkets of all kinds
and another blanket.

I made the only response I knew, and all my
trembling lips could be made to say, *"Le lila waste.
Pi la ya kia."* ("This is beautiful. My thanks I
give you.")

Somehow I sensed the fact that, although I had
thus been honored among them, they would prefer
to have the rest of their celebration unwitnessed
by me. I suggested this to the Government teacher
and her escort, who were with me, and we left
shortly. I could not sleep for the incessant tom-
toms that beat until morning. They must have
beaten out dance after dance like mine, for the
noise quieted at intervals when, I suppose, they
bestowed other eagle feathers and blankets and led
in other ponies.

The Government teacher was terribly frightened
by the night's experience, and talked of leaving.

I did what was doubtless the worst thing I could have done. I told her about White Blanket in my wish to protect her from a similar experience. She rushed to her room and barred the door. During my entire stay at Cut Meat Creek she would bolt herself in if she saw any Indian man, regardless of his age or the direction in which he was going.

CHAPTER ELEVEN

THE school at Cut Meat Creek Camp was for children. We two teachers occupied a Government-erected log house which was comfortable. The large square front room was the schoolroom. Back of it were three rooms in a row, a living room, a kitchen, and a sleeping room. At first we shared the sleeping room, but my companion insited that she was too scared to get up at night and mend the fires, and also grumbled because I disturbed her when I did it, so, for the sake of peace, I soon moved my cot into the kitchen. Our wood and water were to be brought to us by boys hired by the Government.

I arrived at Cut Meat Camp in time to plant the garden and flower seeds which my father had sent me. I hired the ground broken with hand tools borrowed from the agency, and planted my garden beside our quarters. I had a big straw hat which Mother had sent me—lest I ruin my complexion. The hat was my chief power. The Indians came and felt of it and examined it to see how it might be made, but paid little heed to how to make a garden. I had radishes, lettuce, onions, turnips, beets, beans, and corn, zinnias and nasturtiums. The young plants in rows elicited some comment. When I demonstrated radishes and lettuce the interest grew. But it was the beans that did the business. Here was a small white woman in a very large hat, unlike anything in the uniform of the medicine man, and she was making as many beans come out of a little piece of ground as the whole village could gather from the mice in a season! My crowning triumph came when my corn stood ten feet high, and I turned back the husks to display fifteen-inch ears of even, golden grains. The medicine man was second to me after that, and all of the Cut Meat Creek Indians put complete faith in all I said. The hat didn't do much for my complexion, but it won me my spurs as perhaps nothing else could have done as a "woman of mighty wisdom."

Inside the house I could demonstrate two sewing machines sent out by the Government. After seeing them the women couldn't be kept away. I was always busy showing them how to fashion their clothing so it would not be so cumbersome in winter and so uncomfortably warm in summer. I went alone up and down the creek to the villages, for which my teaching partner always soundly berated me, quite as elegantly as Mother might have done. She said I was perfectly "foolhardy the way I traipsed around alone with all the woman-stealing young bucks watching me from the plum brush."

I had night school every weekday night in the big room for the grownups. Perhaps it was one of the first adult-education projects in America. Though it was for grownups, the parents brought their babies and children with them. Everybody sat patiently through the lesson hour, but they really unbent when I offered them steaming coffee and red apples. It was a conglomeration of human beings who came to my school; there was always more or less confusion, but I managed somehow to get the elements of numbers and reading into many a graying head. They never ceased to marvel at one who could count by groups other than ones or tens. I believe that arithmetic, next to geography, the Indians found most wonderful.

My art study stood me in good stead. I could sketch an object and beneath it write their name for it along with the English. They soon commanded enough English so that they attempted to talk to me in my own tongue. They doted on these sketches as children might, and gave me unspoken homage for an ability which seemed marvelous to them. The children who had come to day school often accompanied their parents, and proudly, if I asked them, would recite all they had learned, would count and sing and read. I did not teach in the day school, but I was in charge of it. I always went in in the morning to play the organ and teach the songs.

Among my night-school pupils was a strikingly handsome young brave of about nineteen. He had traded a pony for a brilliant red and purple silk handkerchief, and always wore it, carefully knotted beneath his chin. He was alert and eager and learned rapidly. One evening he was accompanied by a stupid-looking old squaw of about sixty. He introduced her as his wife. Foolishly I blurted out what was in my mind: "Why, Two Horns," I said, "This woman is at least old enough to be your grandmother!"

"No difference," he replied easily. "Let me write the fifty and six and the forty and two more first, tonight." Thus was I shown my place!

Though some Cheyennes lived here with the Teton Sioux, they respected each other's wives and property. There was no thieving or wife-stealing. Some of them were divorced—by mutual consent. The divorced man usually left the village, the wife retaining the tepee and all it contained—including the children—and the husband taking the cattle and horses. There was no quarreling.

The men here sat around most of the time, talking. I used to walk slowly by groups thus occupied to find out what subject it might be that was so inexhaustible. This was none too easy to do, for they always stopped all talk when I approached, and I got only the loudest voices, which could be heard at a distance. I was still not very sure of the language, this Teton Sioux, mixed and mingled as it was with Cheyenne.

Much to my amusement I found that this important thing which prevented the men from turning a hand to the lifting, tugging, hauling and child tending which left the squaws no leisure, was just about as important as the conversation one might expect to hear from a street meeting of small boys in their first long trousers. The speeches varied, but they were all just "blurbs"—personal blurbs. They would go on something like this: "Here"— accompanied by a prodigious thumping of the chest—"I—I—many good things I do. I am strongest with the battle club and can shoot down the fleetest buffalo. My arrow cannot miss. I ride without returning farther than any. If my pony tries all his art he cannot get me from his back. . . ." and on and on, each with a little different simile, but with identical content.

I believe that they did not waste their time altogether, but actually stayed themselves for future test by reiterating a prowess which they, repeating thus often, came to look on as fact.

I attended one of their councils. The Indian council has been so widely written of that I can add nothing except perhaps to say that these men counciled not about war, but about peace: where the herds should be pastured next, when and where they should go on the next hunt, if the camp had food enough to last to a stated time, census of the tribe's cattle and ponies. They closed their business by smoking the peace pipe. It was passed from man to man, each taking a whiff before he passed it on to be returned to the chief who had started it on its journey around the circle of cross-legged men.

These men hunted and trapped much of the time in winter and brought in deer and bear. They had many buffalo robes and skulls, and talked much of buffalo, but I saw no buffalo while I was at the camp. They piled up the pelts of mink, weasel, coyote, and gray timber wolf beside their tepees, and twice a year carried them to the Government station to trade them for iron pots and laundry tubs and the cotton cloth of ciivlization. They wore tomahawks and knives and even war clubs at their belts. Each man always carried his bow and arrows. On their winter hunting trips they wrapped their legs in more hides than usual and wore heavy buckskin shirts.

By now I had learned to ride with both skill and endurance, and I galloped out over the trailless prairies and up and down the canyons to visit, leave medicine, and trade. Unconsciously I was becoming one of them, for I loved the wild freedom and recalled with a smile the academy at Georgetown where rules had held young growing girls indoors morning, noon, and night. The Indian girl was not so closely watched, for her curfew rang at sunset

and the Mt. Holyoke curfew had been reported to
be at six.

Mother's letters were friendlier and more sympathetic, for she wrote:

> I have grown very thin so that I cannot wear any but my
> new dress. If I came to Dakota I might get fat as you have
> done. I am sending you a collar for your little dog. Papa
> punched more holes in it so you could make it fit. It's just
> like Beppo's. Why can't you raise chickens? From what you
> say, the soil must be as rich as right here in Washington. . . .
> My new dress has pasementry trimming on black satin. . . .

I had been glad to prove my speech to Father.
I had grown a garden, had "shown them how."
Next year the Indians planted gardens and, as far
as I know, remained there and stopped roving.
Cut Meat Creek Camp certainly took on a new
look that next year, and I was thoroughly happy.

The Government wagons brought grief. It became apparent that the trips to the agency were
becoming more and more frequent. After each trip
there was to be expected the spectacle of drunken
Indians. They began to gamble openly among the
tepees, and the women worked harder than ever
and had less to eat. There were many log houses
by now. When one morning I found new glass
windows missing from the last house built, I gave
myself a new job. I went on secret service, self-
appointed.

It was only a few days later that I came upon a
group of men gambling with plum pits. The

CHEYENNE MEDICINE SONG

CHEYENNE MEDICINE SONG
(translation)

I go by night unseen on my way.
Then am I holy;
Then have I power to make well the sick.

DAKOTA MEDICINE SONG

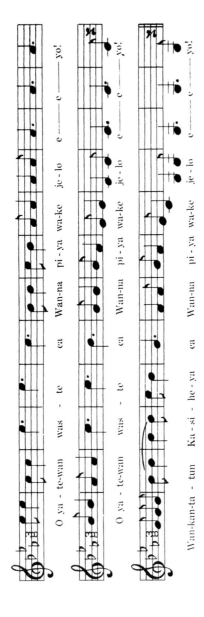

DAKOTA MEDICINE SONG
(translation)

Now all, now all, be healed.
New life shall be yours
Through the Great Mystery, healed.

stakes were laundry tubs and glass windows—
worthless things meant only to help women. I
stepped into their midst.

"*Kikilupi!*" ("Get back!") said the leader, "Get
away white woman! We don't want you!"

Without moving, I answered, "Get those tubs
and windows back by tomorrow or I will see that
you go to the guardhouse." That was that, and the
things were returned to their proper places.

A German trader was responsible for the sudden
inflow of whiskey. I had no proof. I just suspected
him. Just before I left Cut Meat Creek I saw him
one day delivering whiskey to two young boys behind one of the remaining tepees. Next day he was
arrested on my testimony, and served his sentence.
I now had two factions against me: the medicine
men who felt that I had stolen their thunder, and
the lazy and shiftless men of the village who wished
to drink and gamble unmolested.

It was at Cut Meat Creek that I saw a medicine
man at close range, administering a cure. His patient looked to be a very sick man, for his eyes were
bright with high fever and he could scarcely stand
unaided. But stand he must, and did, until the
healer heated two stones which he then lugged inside
of a tiny tepee which might hold two men if they
weren't too fat. The doctor brought water and
poured on the hot stones. He disrobed his patient
and thrust him unceremoniously into the tent

which was filled with steam. He set more stones to heat. But the steam stopped forming, and the man became chilled so ,he was forced by his physician to run rapidly about outside the tepee until the second lot of stones should heat hot enough to produce steam from water poured upon them. Brutal as the treatment appeared to be, the patient was able to dress and walk back unaided to his own tepee after paying his bill with pigeon eggs and beads.

The women said this medicine man could rub out "evil spirits" with his hands, but he usually contented himself with bitter concoctions to pour down the throat. Many Indians in the camps around died from tuberculosis and some sort of scrofulous infection, produced, I thought, from their using the flesh of dogs as food—the same dogs who were the sanitation scavengers of the camps before being killed for food.

CHAPTER TWELVE

I HAD to be constantly on the alert now for the medicine men and the gamblers, but my war finally came from a wholly unexpected quarter. Old Yellow Hat, one of the dirtiest fellows in camp, took to coming to the children's day school and listening with close attenton. He had been called Yellow Hat because he wore, summer and winter, a dirty old yellow head covering of mangy fox fur. He lived in one of the outlying tepees and kept the filthiest quarters of any Indian I have ever known. Besides his tepee, he also had a ramshackle house which was graced by a white man's stove from the agency store. With him lived some twenty or more children and grandchildren, a flock of chickens, and a bigger flock of pigeons. I had bought pigeon eggs of him often.

My assistant said he always came in, sat down, and said nothing, but listened intently and watched everything like a hawk. She was downright afraid of him. I always knew when he went away, for he invariably came, unannounced, according to Indian custom, into our private quarters. He came to beg, usually chalk or pencils.

One day he stuck his frowsy head into the kitchen where I was at work and asked me if I would "do him much good." I at once put down my work and listened. He wanted, he said, to "know what is horse, English." By the time I had given him the English words for all the common things about camp he had quite a lengthy list. At his request I had written the information down for him. He went away, grunting contentedly. He had folded the paper and stowed it in the jumble of clothing under his chin. He walked off towards his tepee, tall, erect, and dignified, an imposing figure when he had gotten far enough away so that his dirt was not visible. He was chief of Cut Meat Creek Camp.

The next day there were no children at school. They were running about and yelling in rich abandonment. I went to the Government Indian police and sent him with a message to Yellow Hat. The message he brought back that was Yellow Hat would henceforth teach the children all their fathers thought needful, that such was not the business of "two little white squaws."

I walked down to Yellow Hat's hut, alone. Inside I saw a blackboard. He had the chalk and pencils he had begged from me. His "book" from which he had taught the children that morning for an hour was the paper list of English words I had written for him.

"Every morning," I said to him in his own tongue, "when the flag is raised at my school, the Great Father at Washington commands that every child shall come to school to be taught. If you refuse to let them, in three days you will be taken to the guardhouse."

He returned not a word. I turned and walked back without once glancing around. Next morning the children came back. He kept the pencils and blackboard and word list, and the pigeons found the blackboard a fine roost. I learned that Yellow Hat often taught his own children and grandchildren from my English list "what their fathers thought needful for them to know." But the children attended my school also.

At Cut Meat Creek we received clothing sent by missionary societies. It became the duty of the teachers to instruct the little boys in the art of the civilized bath and to show them how to put on civilized clothing. They objected with all the power they could muster. Hair was the first battlefield. Not by any argument could they be persuaded to have their long, rancid scalp locks cut. The rest of their hair fell about their shoulders and was dirty, unkempt, and ill-smelling. From first to last they clung to their hair, but we finally compromised by trimming all but the scalp lock. They looked comical enough after the operation with their long scalp locks erupting from nicely clipped heads. It made it possible for us to teach them to keep their heads clean.

When a clothing box arrived and was opened, the boys would crowd around, fingering and eyeing and snatching at their choices, as any small boy might. They were keen at this. Once a boy had chosen his suit and I had said that he might have it, he renewed his search through what remained in the box and was back in no time with a second outfit to ask my assent. They could not understand keeping a reserve supply.

One by one we took them into our quarters and introduced them to a tub of warm, soapy water beside a glowing stove. The washcloth completely mystified them. They had had a hurried council in the schoolroom when baths had been described and proposed. "Are you going to?" they had asked each other. The answer had been, usually, "No, that white woman could look at me." Although Indians lived in one tepee together, they were all modest to a degree, and always managed to disrobe beneath a blanket, never unscreened. This idea of public disrobing was against all tradition.

After explaining how to bathe, we left the room and hoped each lad would do a good job of it, but when we found that their efforts consisted chiefly in examining the soap, washcloth, and tub, we rolled up our sleeves and scrubbed little red necks and ears and bodies. Then came the underwear:

long-sleeved and long-legged fleeced union suits. To our profound relief the boys liked these immensely, and considered them sufficient clothing in the house. When we showed them themselves in a mirror, and they saw how fine they looked in both suits, an inner and an outer one, they were eager to wear all of this white man's clothing.

The children ate dinner at school. We teachers provided it, such as it was: one piece of Government hardtack, one slice of wheat bread spread with jelly, one tin cup of hot coffee with sugar and cream. It was the best we could do, and the children were more than happy with these strange delicacies. I taught the older girls to bake the bread. We set sponge at night, and I protected it by my kitchen fire until morning. The girl whose turn it was to do the baking came early. None of them ever failed, though early mornings were cruelly cold. The bread was baked by lunchtime, and the odor of the bread and coffee, I believe, inspired many a stubborn little heart to master the lesson which must precede the school "feast."

There were many deer about Cut Meat Creek. In the depth of winter when one snow had followed on the heels of another, I witnessed a scene that I often recall. It was sharp, cold starlight. I was enjoying the beauty of it from my window just before retiring, when a shadowy group moved out from the creek timber and advanced timidly to-

wards the village. As they came nearer I saw that
they were deer. They followed their antlered
leader right to the dooryards of the tepees, where
they pawed at the snow which had been somewhat
softened by the heat from the fires within. For a
long time they fed upon the grass they uncovered,
for the dogs were all in the tepees, and there was
not a sound to startle them. At last one dog in a
near-by tepee must have been awakened by the
pawing hoofs, or scented the deer, for he let out a
howl which was answered by every dog in the village. The deer bounded away and disappeared. I
have never seen a more beautiful thing than their
graceful, nimble flight across the snow.

The Indians had balls of their own manufacture,
larger than a baseball, stitched from oddly shaped
pieces and stuffed with hair or fur. When I arrived
at Cut Meat Creek—and I was the first white person to live among them—the boys and men both
spent much time playing ball, a game of skill in
throwing and catching. The children threw the
balls over the tepees to each other in real "ante-
over" style. They snowballed each other and built
high columns out of snow. They were not snow
men but imitations of totem poles. The children
called them "toto." They smoothed the sides evenly
and pricked designs from top to bottom and further ornamented the motifs of the designs with
bits of fur, rabbits' tails, and feathers. They also

DAKOTA SWING SONG

played hockey with a crooked stick, using the knob of some animal's ball-and-socket joint. The littlest fellows played tag and hid from each other. The boys at our school played leapfrog, a game in which they were often joined by their fathers after school hours.

I always had much trouble with the boys, for they wanted to do all the talking in the schoolroom. When we attempted to seat the boys and girls promiscuously we were met by half a dozen angry little men.

"You talk too much," the leader flung at us.

I recited patiently that I had to talk if I taught. I finally won them by this little speech: "Do you not see that when you talk to me I use my ears and listen? Then, when I talk to you you must use your ears and listen. Now, I will tell you how to play. ..." and I initiated them into the game of drop the handkerchief. They romped and played and shouted. "Now," I said, "if you had not used your ears and listened you would not have learned how to have so much fun, would you?"

We knew we were fighting tradition as old as the race, for the men talked constantly in the tepees in loud, braggart voices. The women talked most of the time, too, but they whispered together. These little boys just could not tolerate the idea of letting a little girl have the floor all to herself to talk loudly the answers they themselves were not sure of. Often they would break in in an extra-loud voice in order to prevent the insult of a woman-child talking out loud and telling something which the man-child did not know.

In casting about for a suitably simple little verse to teach them, I attempted the classic beginning, "I love little pussy her coat is so warm." I got no farther.

"No good cat-talk," one youth prompted me. "Bear-talk good."

So it went. The boys didn't want the girls to go on fruit-hunting expeditions. They sulked if I asked a girl to answer a question they had missed. And, of all things, how could a self-respecting Indian boy be expected to maintain his self-respect if he were obliged to count *with* the "weak women?" By degrees, the novel things of the schoolroom won over these dominating little males, and our sessions were less stormy. The children learned rapidly.

Most of the women here were slovenly workers. They were charmed by the big shining dishpans to be gotten at the agency, and relegated their own iron pots and pottery vessels to the junk pile in favor of these light new miraculous pans. Laundering, bathing, cooking—all were often accomplished in one and the same pan! So I tried to dwell on cleanliness in my bread-baking class at school. Bread would never rise, I said, unles the pan was spotless.

CHAPTER THIRTEEN

IN the night school I had a difficult time, also. For I was bold enough to preach the doctrine of a more equal division of labor. It was uphill going, and I cannot forget the injured and comical looks exchanged by the men when I dwelt upon this mode of improving woman's lot. Once I was gratified to hear an old squaw bragging to her neighbor that her man was "red man good and white man good, too." He had helped her with the wood. The women always bragged among themselves about their husbands—a kind of echo of the masculine bragging. They took definite pains to array their males in their cleverest hand-work. In this direction there was keen competition among them.

The child called its mother "Ina," its father "Ata." One heard Ina oftenest, for the father paid little attention to his child until the son began to grow long legs. How proud was such a lad to be spoken to by his father! He offered all manner of service to gain attention: "Shall I take your horses to the river?" If given the privilege, he would run off completely happy. He knew that now Ata looked upon his horsemanship with approval.

My little homily to these men went something like this: "You know much your wives do not know. Your wives can do much you cannot do. They could not live without the kill you bring to them. You would freeze without the tepee they make so pleasant when the harsh winter is here. To kill the food is no more needful than to be kept from freezing." Occasionally I saw a flicker of response to my logic in some seamed and puzzled face.

One day my assistant neglected to remind the boys that our wood and water supply was low. Though they had been hired by the Government and had had their duties amply explained, they always had to be reminded. We didn't have fuel enough to last the night. It was so dismally cold, all of our supplies would freeze without fire, and we had a few precious apples in the supply box.

"Hold the lamp for me," I said to Minnie, the assistant teacher, "and I'll just run out and bring in enough to last until morning."

For answer, Minnie ran into her room and bolted the door. I remembered my experience at Elizabeth's, for Minnie was haranguing behind her door about white blankets and wife-stealers and the rest of her usual speech. The only way to save our food was to get wood. I opened the door and looked out.

The village lay sound asleep. There was not a sound of any kind, not the least crackle of a twig. I dashed out and got the wood. When I straightened up with my armload there stood the dreaded White Blanket. He caught me with one swoop, but I clung to my wood, and that made his problem a little difficult. I did not struggle, but asked evenly, "What do you want?"

"Tado un pejuta sapa siyo" ("Meat and black medicine-coffee") he said, loosing his hold on me a trifle.

"All right," I said, making no move to get away, "but this little bit of wood I have will not be enough to cook meat and medicine-coffee, too. Bring some more and I will cook for you."

He released me instantly. I wanted to run, but I knew that would lose the day, so I walked as calmly as I could back to the house. When I reached the door, which still stood open, I dashed inside, dropped the wood, and slammed and bolted the door. White Blanket, who had been leisurely stacking wood upon his arm, dropped the wood and raced up just as I drew the bolt. He banged on the door. "Blue Star, I will get much wood!"

"My clock says it is too late to cook tonight," I called back. "Come back in the morning and I will give you meat and much good medicine-coffee."

He burst into angry whoops and went about the house, shaking the windows and yelling horribly.

He came back to the schoolroom window and called, "Come here, Blue Star." He was holding up something for me to see. I caught the glitter of a ring.

"Come back tomorrow," I said, "and I will look at it."

His anger was redoubled. He froze my blood with his whoops. But he went off at last, emitting his hideous cries as he went. He did not come back the next day.

But next day Minnie packed her possessions and left for home before dinner. She had all and more than she wanted of this "Indian teaching business." I was thus left alone with all the teaching and nursing and night-school problems—and this new suitor. Since the day was Saturday I decided to ride the seven miles to the nearest camp school which had just been established under the direction of a George and Belle Douglas. Since George had ridden in, leading a pony for my return trip, I accepted gratefully. My entertainment that day consisted of riding out with George to search for a horse that had strayed. Belle was not well, so she did not ride, but prepared a fine lunch for us to take along. I had become an Indian so far as clothing was concerned. I wore long heavy leather leggings and boots and a skin coat and cap. It was sharp and cold, but pleasant.

We headed in the direction in which the horse

had last been seen, our ponies trotting easily over the low trailless hills. I had become great friends with these people and often rode over to spend week ends, after having provided Minnie with a squaw as bodyguard. We talked as we rode, and I recounted the experience of the night before. Mr. Douglas seemed much disturbed, and said with decision that it would never do for me to try to go on alone after such an experience in that place. I saw, too, how foolhardy it would be, and hoped the agency would send a more courageous aid than Minnie had been.

Off to the northwest we saw a mounted figure approaching. He proved to be a Crow Indian. Mr. Douglas inquired in the sign language about his strayed horse. By signs the Crow directed us towards a wooded slope of the river about five miles farther down. We searched without finding the pony until near sundown when we came upon her and her newborn colt. When Mr. Douglas dismounted, the pony rushed him with bared teeth and sent him headlong back to his saddle. By both of us maneuvering her we at last got her headed for home. Twenty miles back! We had not gone more than a mile when the colt lay down and refused to rise. I kept close to the mother and between her and Mr. Douglas while he lifted the colt to his saddle. We trotted briskly off, and the pony followed.

I returned to Cut Meat Camp, only to leave at once, and permanently. The agent could find no one to take Minnie's place, and it was thought too risky for me to stay alone. I made no answer to this decision: Minnie had been such a staunch protector!

I remained for some weeks at the home of the agent as his guest before I conceived the idea of making a speaking tour in the Indians' behalf. I hoped to raise enough money to build and equip a school of my own as a school should be equipped. Even after I had stumped most of the Middle Western states and had obtained some small gifts and promises for larger ones, there was still no opening for me.

Uncle Thomas Updegraff, who was living at Macgregor, Iowa, urged me to come to his home for a month's stay. It seemed strange, indeed, to be party going again, and to be dancing and boat riding in the midst of civilization. This was my second vacation since going to Dakota, and I enjoyed it thoroughly, but when the letter came offering me a position at Fort Bennett, I cut my visit short and started West by the first train.

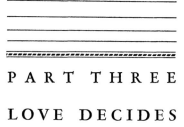

PART THREE

LOVE DECIDES

CHAPTER FOURTEEN

AT the Indian school near Fort Bennett I was put in charge of thirty-six little boys of from six to twelve years of age. They were circumspect in all they did, and rarely needed direction of any kind. I had been at Fort Bennett but a few days when measles broke out in the school. Instead of teaching, I was drafted as a nurse. I sat among them in the dormitory where they lay two in a bed and talked to them, told them stories, and eased them as best I could. All of them were very ill, one little fellow was dangerously so, I realized.

As I sat beside him one night he asked repeatedly for one of the older boys. His fever-brightened eyes were so pleading that I sent for Bold Eagle—against the rules. I held the little boy in my arms while we waited for his big friend to arrive and I tried to comfort him with the Sioux lullaby I knew so well. He began hemorrhaging and died in a few minutes, though Bold Eagle came in in time to be recognized. The child had not complained at all. I straightened his little body and pulled the sheet over it smoothly. Was it wise, I wondered, to take such little ones from home? Still children died every winter in the camps from measles.

His mother and father came to claim the body. Though in all my experience I never witnessed the funeral of a child or woman, I now witnessed the touching grief of Indian parents as they stood looking down upon the little dead face. Silently the mother stooped, lifted the rigid form, and walked out with bowed head, followed by the father. The other patients were wide-eyed, but no one said anything.

The boys were slow in recovering, but in due time I returned to my desk. They were interested and industrious. There was no hubbub about girls' place, for there were no girls in this school. The little boys took my gender and authority as much a matter of course as they did their own mother's.

Each boy had been permitted to bring his pony to the school. We had great fun racing together, for I loved racing and rode well enough to race the best of them. I helped plan and make the garden. We harvested the cabbage, beets, and potatoes together. I even drove a hayrake in the fields. I enjoyed that thoroughly and became expert at piling even windrows. I began to think about owning some of this fertile land, and dreamed of flocks and herds, as my father had dreamed before me.

My one relaxation was riding in to the post office,

a trip I made daily. Besides an enormous corres-
pondence, I wrote regularly for some of the church
periodicals, columns about Indians, drawn from my
experiences and observation. I was fond of writing,
and became an easy, if not eloquent scribe. I wrote
long letters home, now mostly filled with my
dreams of becoming a farmer.

One day as I approached the post office by way
of the bridge, I met a handsome young man. He
was sunburned, and his face bore traces of Indian
ancestry, but his clothing and mien were that of
an English gentleman. Not long after this first
meeting I was introduced to him, Samuel Campbell. He was the son of a trader and a Sioux Indian
woman. His mother had died when he was young,
and he had been reared by the Episcopal clergyman
of the little church at Fort Bennett, and had taken
his foster father's name. We rode and talked together, and fell in love.

In the autumn I was sent to Swift Bird's camp,
seventy-five miles from the fort. Swift Bird was a
wise chief. He had evaluated the white man's education and his manner of living and had decided
that both were superior to his own. He sent his
sons and daughters to Government schools. Although his village was called a camp, it had few
tepees. Most of the families were housed in well-
built structures. The schoolhouse was a two-story
building, the second floor being set aside as the

teacher's quarters. It was reached by an outside
stair. In a separate log room the Government had
fitted up a school kitchen with a stove and cooking
utensils. I was to be alone here, but I felt no fear
at all, and placed my personal belongings about my
cozy living room. Tending the fires in kitchen,
schoolroom, and living quarters devolved upon me
—no small task. Mr. Campbell rode over for the
week end and put up at a friend's house. We rode
to a neighboring camp to attend church, out
across the prairie, off the trails. The country here
was flat and uninteresting, but we dismounted to
watch the prairie dogs with which the whole country was infested. These Indians did not care for
prairie-dog meat, and the fur was of little value.
When cold weather set in we drove a bobsled on the
frozen river to Chargus' Camp or White Horse
Camp to see William and Rebecca Holmes, a couple
who served the Episcopal Church thirty miles up
the river.

One Communion Sunday we had gone into this
little church and were kneeling with the other communicants, when an old Indian entered. He
sniffed appreciatively. When his eye caught the
wine cup being passed around, he knelt in direct
line of its passage and drained it when it came to
him. The young minister was at a loss as to what
to do, but he refilled it and set it again on its interrupted round. The Indian rose, knelt again, and

drained the cup. There was no more wine. The last communicants did without. Now the old fellow appraised the warm stove, stepped up to it, and with copious grunts warmed himself. Comfortable at last, he sat down, filled his pipe with kinnikinnick, and smoked throughout the sermon.

At Swift Bird's Camp my water was to be hauled by High Bear. I had a barrel with a charcoal strainer at the top, which he was to fill every day. He contrived a carrier from a forked branch and other uprights fastened to a rude sledge. The uprights kept the barrel from sliding off the sledge when it was hauled over the ruts of the riverbank by the two ponies hitched to it by leather thongs. The river was swift, and villages distant, so I thought the water uncontaminated. This barrel of water supplied the children for drinking as well as supplying my domestic needs. But one day the barrel was not filled.

The Friday before, I had had an impromptu program, as I always had, in an attempt to bring out these shy children. Each chose what he wished to do, and usually was eager and proud to do it. At recess High Bear's son had come to me before the others had settled themselves in their seats and said, "Ugh, me first!"

"Yes," I told him, "of course you may"—for he had been one of the most backward ones. "But wait until all are in their seats."

"Two Horns will speak first today," I announced.

The boy evidently had not heard.

"Two Horns is going to speak now," I said, much louder. "Come on, Two Horns." I tried several other formulas, but from the dead quiet of the room I knew that Two Horns had had his mighty dignity offended by being made to wait.

"*El na ja wo!*" ("Get up, right now!") I said sternly.

Not a twitch of a muscle, even; he might have been a statue.

"Runs the Enemy," I said, "go outside and bring me a long (measuring) piece of a tree." There was an audible gasp. Indians do not punish their children.

I pulled Two Horns from his seat and switched his legs soundly. He made no sound, offered no resistance, and sat back in his seat, a statue still, without expression of any kind.

"When I call you to come, Two Horns, next time, you are to come and speak," I said. I had every child up. The program progressed with unusual speed. Then I called Two Horns. He rose, came to his place, chucking his chin into his shirt and hunching his shoulders nearly double, he mumbled perhaps two sentences. The children tittered. Monday he was not at school, and my water barrel was not filled.

United States Indian Service,

Cheyenne River Agency.

September 26th, 1887

No

Miss Fellows,

Teacher No. 4 Day School

Swift Birds Camp –

I send you by team leaving this morning – 6 Hand Grenades, for the protection of the School building, and which in case of fire are to broken so that the contents will fall in the fire – Also I send you

1 Teachers desk Complete
1 Wash Boiler
5 gall Coal Oil –
4 Chairs
1 Iron Rake
1 Axe & handle
1 Clasp, & 2 Staples
2 qts Varnish for School desks (red)
200 lbs. Flour 50 lbs Sugar 25 lbs. Coffee x
1½ lb. Baking Powder for Lunch for School

Official Letter to Corabelle Fellows

United States Indian Service,

Cheyenne River Agency,

Nov. 28th, 1885.

Miss Fellows,

Madam:

Swift Bird will be instructed to say to send his daughter Edith to School.

If you cannot regulate the attendance at your School, you can discontinue it at once.

The school room and your apartments are under your entire control, and you must make your rules and enforce them.

Very respectfully

Chas E. McChesney

U.S. Agent

Per C.R.W.

Official Letter to Corabelle Fellows

No water had been brought on Saturday or Sunday. I had carried what I needed. Monday night I answered the door to find Runs the Enemy (Sr.), Indian police, who offered me the information that High Bear had sent him to say that nobody but the chief may punish children. I had heard that these people sent their unmanageable children to the chief, who, so far as I know, never punished them. He only upbraided them for not being "men with good hearts." I knew the women did not punish. I had heard them say to a disobedient child, "I shall talk a great deal to your father about this," which was usually powerful enough to achieve immediate obedience. I had never seen a father punish his child, nor had I heard a child cry as if from punishment.

Wednesday, High Bear came in person.

"*Itaska, winyn nasula,*" ("White-faced woman has no brains"), he said sullenly.

"I am sent by the Great Father at Washington to teach the children," I replied.

"Ugh! *Can scotta hoksila!*" ("Oh, but you played on my child with the long wood!")

"The way of the Great Father is not your way," I said. "I teach all of the children. I do not have time to wait until they want to talk. You can wait when you have but one child."

"Ugh! *Can scotta hoksila!*"

"Tell your little boy," I said, "if he will rise up

and speak when I call him that I will not play on him with the long wood."

Two Horns came back to school. I gave him two—not one—hardtack crackers to show him that I was not his enemy. One day he brought me a gift, a tiny whitewood canoe he himself had carved. Two Horns and I were friends, and he recited when I called on him.

I had many gifts from these children, canoes mostly from the boys, and little patches of beaded skin from the girls. The Indian parents taught their children what they would need to know to carry on the life of the tribe. The chief's wife sometimes brought me gifts—newly fried Dakota bread, or a cooked quail. Indian women, like all other women, vary in personal cleanliness. I ate the gifts of the chief's wife with relish, for I knew her to be an orderly and cleanly housewife.

I nearly precipitated civil war when I attempted to call each child in the family by the father's name. The men stormed the schoolroom, wagging their heads fiercely and vociferously repeating, "*Hecca tu sni!*" ("This is all a mistake!") I had to talk fast about the Great Father at Washington and mention my own relative who sat under the same lodge skin with the Great Father and made laws concerning names. My pupils here, as their names appeared, after I had given them a first English name, I take from an old envelope. Paper was hard to get. I used every scrap that came my way. The list reads: David, Eli, Luther, Aaron, and Joseph Broken Leg; Ed, Isaac, William, and May Grayhound; Frank and Harry Jumping Eagle; Tom and James Turning Eagle; Moses High Lance; Elmer and Nell Fast Dog; Victor Coyote; Milo and Dora Barkside; John Sharp Tail; Paul, Clark, and Edgar Sitting Bear; Isaac Yellow Robe; Ida and Ella Old Medicine; Rosa With Horns; Phoebe and Ann Three Bears; Cora Many Holes; Fanny Deep Bear; Elizabeth, Mable, and Sam Runs the Enemy.

Though these Indians had cattle, they had never used milk and did not know how to make butter. I could not obtain a churn, so I experimented with a tin pail that had a cover. It was hard work, but after shaking the cream back and forth in it I was rewarded with a little pat of butter. The women learned the trick, and I could not have been more awesomely honored had I raised one of their departed braves from the dead. They named butter "grease of milk."

I was able, from my study of a "doctor book" presented to me by the Presbyterian Church in Washington, to identify many of the concoctions of the medicine men. They looked upon me in alarm, particularly when I questioned them or named something which they were using as medicine. The women had great faith in me and often would come tap-tapping softly at my window to say, "My child—it is much, much too hot," or "My child—his cheek is much, much too big." I always went with them to try to ease the little sufferer, and usually was able to do so. Any disease which spotted the skin they called "spotted fever."

My treatment was usually a dose of castor oil, with warm or cold sponge baths. Women who treated their own children for measles, took them once a day—if it was not too bitterly cold—to the river, where they bathed them, then took them back into the tepee, where they rubbed them from head to foot with grease—snake oil or skunk oil, preferably. Snake oil was considered good for measles, mumps, and whooping cough. The women also brewed herb teas of many kinds and must have had a fair knowledge of the plants which they gathered and dried for that purpose. For rheumatism they used snakeroot. They chewed wild flag as a laxative. The medicine men used mandrake for the scrofula, with which many of the older men were afflicted. They must have died hideous deaths before the white man came. Now they were using "blue vitriol" packs made of chemical gotten at the agency. Kinnikinnick, sage, onions, and oxalis were used as teas and to bathe wounds.

CHAPTER FIFTEEN

SINCE my fiancé lived at Fort Bennett, I could not spend my vacation there without flouting Indian morality. Instead, I accepted the invitation of Good Dog to go with him and his family on a round of visits.

I had my own feather bed, blanket, and pillow. During the two weeks while we went from camp to camp I had no bath. The river water was too cold for me to bathe in as the Indians did, and I was never free from the possibility of interruption in the tepee. So they were cleaner than I. Since I had not mastered the art of undressing under a blanket, I was obliged to sleep in my clothes.

Good Dog had but one wife. I scarcely heard a sound from their two little boys during the entire two weeks, certainly no complaining or quarreling. I was assigned the place of honor opposite the entrance because of my "brave heart and wisdom." I did comb my hair often and wash my face often. This impressed Good Dog's wife. She stroked my hair when I let it down, and admired it, it was so much finer and better cared for than her own. I showed her the art of hair shampooing. She was

intrigued with my hairpins and my tiny sifter can
of talcum powder.

At one Indian village we were awakened after
midnight by loud cheerful talk, just outside. The
proverbial fatted calf had been killed in my honor,
and the preparation for the feast was in progress.
The men were doing the cooking!

Someone raised the tepee flap. "Rise up, Blue
Star," said a strange voice. "You need not sleep
because it is dark. Rise up, we have much meat for
you."

I was a little frightened, but when Good Dog
appeared also at the flap and repeated the invitation
I rose, made what toilet I might, and went out.
It was pleasant to sit before the roaring fire. The
meat, cut in strips, was broiling on sharp sticks
and sending out a delicious odor. Many men and
women sat about, and I took my place with the
rest and ate from my fingers the rather rare meat
served me—first. Before me rushed the picture of
my mother's dining room, of shortcakes and loin
roasts, linen, flowers, and finger bowls. I felt keenly
my need of a bath, my ill-arranged hair, my wrin-
kled clothing. I remembered the little flatiron.
With something like consternation I realized how
keenly I was enjoying myself, almost one with these
Indians. That I was doing their way, not they mine.

The men laughed and talked loudly and with
abandon. The women jabbered as usual. I sat

solemnly considering my future among these people. I was affianced to an educated man, who, however, had Indian blood. I wondered if a generation
or two of education could change completely the
age-old Indian tradition of man and wife, of
cleanliness, of interest in affairs outside the village.

My thoughts were interrupted. The crowning
delicacy of the feast was going round, kinnikinnick
tea, served in bright new agency tin cups. It was
unsweetened, but it was hot and savory and not
unpleasant. What, after all, was the difference between these people and, say, my mother? They
were anxious to learn all that my race knew which
theirs did not. My mother was sure that they had
nothing of the intellect or heart which she would
wish to know. Yet their friendship was the most
vital thing I had yet experienced. There was no
quarreling, no carping, no greed, no grasping.
They toadied to their chief not as much as my
mother toadied to her social leaders. They gos-
siped—not at all. Dawn was reddening when the
party broke up. I felt an eerie sense of impending
disaster, but, after another nap, I was able to laugh
at my midnight soliloquy, and completed the last
few days of the trip with much enjoyment.

After this vacation I returned to routine teaching. I had bought several animals, for I had begun
to build up my equipment for that farm dream.
I had a fine dog, Mazeppa, named from my Byron-

memorizing past. She stayed indoors and slept by
my cot at night. Her companionship kept me from
loneliness, and her fidelity kept out fear of white
blankets. Indians are afraid of dogs. I owned two
ponies, Bess and Prince. I owned a yoke of young
oxen. I cared for these animals myself, and earned
their food. My chickens froze the first winter.
Every morning I drove my stock down to the river,
cut the ice, and let them drink. I hired a guard
fence put around my feed stacks which I placed
northwest of the little barn which was already
built. Father wrote, "What are you trying to do?
Start a Wild West show?"

One night I sat up later than usual, making out
my school reports, when Mazeppa suddenly roused
up and began howling. Between her yowls I could
distinguish the distant sound of lowing cattle.
Range cattle often fled to the settlements during
heavy storms, and this night a blizzard was on. I
knew that Swift Bird's Camp had a strong double
guard about the feed stacks, but I wondered if my
weak one would withstand such an onslaught as
this clamorous lowing promised. I had only a few
tons of hay in my little enclosure, but there were
no more funds in my budget for hay. I was receiving but fifty dollars a month, paid quarterly, and
feed and food were high.

The lowing came closer and closer and, from the
window, I could make out shadowy forms throng-

ing about the main stacks. The cattle were bellowing now, angry at not being able to break the guard.
Now they were heading for my little stack!

Mazeppa and I rushed out and charged them.
They fled bellowing, but as soon as we came indoors,
they returned to the stack guard. After several
charges I decided to sleep in the stacks all night.
With an armload of blankets and a hot stone, I
crawled into the hay. I didn't sleep much for having to run out every little while to chase the cattle
off, but I was snug between trips. Towards morning the cattle moved on down the river, and I
finished my night in bed. When I woke late, I
found that Mazeppa was not in the room. I remembered sleepily that she had not come to the
house with me. I called and whistled, but she did
not come. I dressed in haste and went in search of
her. I found her snuggled into the far side of the
stack where I had stationed her, with nine squirm-
ing new babies.

I wrote father of my night in the hay. He
answered at once:

We imagined blizzards and cyclones and every possible
catastrophe when your letter failed to come on the usual day.
But such lengths as you went to over that hay! Your fence
should be *strong* enough to make such doings unnecessary. If
it is the agent's duty, he has come short of it. If the Indians
should do it, require it of them. If yourself, do not collect hay
until *after* a good fence is up. . . . Your package of curiosities
came. The skins have a familiar look and remind me of boy-

hood. . . . Congress is in session, but doing nothing as usual. . . .
Your mamma has the new member from Lake Erie on the
fourth floor. He talks of going home Christmas to his wife
and nine children. . . .

After I wrote her of my pony, Bess, Mother
wrote:

I am sending you a new dress. Be careful of that pony—
you will break your neck, yet. . . . Do be careful of your complexion. . . .

I had bought Bess unbroken for twenty-five
dollars. Dog Bear brought her around to the school
and said he would help me break her. I held the
lead rope while he attempted to bridle her. When
he sprang to her back she was terrified and worked
for half an hour to get this strange load off. She
reared, stiff-legged, she bucked, she neighed, she
galloped wildly. He stuck on and brought her back
to where I stood with my red saddle. He strapped
the saddle tightly and told me to mount. I sprang
up quickly. She went into the air, and I landed on
the fifth step. The saddle girth had burst. I got
up and remounted her without a saddle. This time
I stuck and rode her several times around the
schoolyard. She soon grew docile and willing.

In the bleak gray mornings I rose, built up three
fires, and cooked my breakfast. Armed with a
tomahawk, I led my animals to the river and
chopped a hole in the ice so they might drink.
After I had them all back in the barn and had fed

them, I did my housework and swept the schoolroom and the school kitchen. Then I was ready to
begin my teaching day.

Near Christmas I bought a bobsled to which I
hitched Prince and Bess and made many a flying
trip about the camp and up and down the river for
fifty miles. It cost heavily to have the ponies
sharpshod, but I was willing to live frugally for
the fine sport of ice driving.

Every Friday afternoon I had a short afternoon
school session so that I might ride to the agency
for my weekly supplies. The trail in led seven
miles over rough hills. When they were snow-cov-
ered the journey was fatiguing for both horse and
rider. Late afternoon of one Friday in January I
fed Prince and the steers, built up the fires, locked
Mazeppa indoors, and mounted Bess, with my bur-
lap sack rolled and tied to the saddle. The air was
damp and stingingly cold, and the wind was rising
as I left.

I hurried Bess over the deeply rutted, snow-cov-
ered trail as fast as she could walk—there was no
chance to canter. I did not stop when I came in
sight of the trader's store, but came on, in spite
of the cold, until I drew up at a small school and
got a list of supplies to be purchased for the Smiths
who kept the school. I dispatched my trading and
theirs and hastened to deliver their parcels. They
were determined that I should eat supper with

them at least, and I, cold and hungry and tired, could not resist their friendly urging.

After the meal I saw the blizzard was coming on in earnest. I hired one of their Indian students to ride ahead and guide me through the storm. The storm increased in intensity until I could scarcely keep to my saddle. At the turn I rode ahead so that his horse might shelter me a little from the wind. After we had ridden some distance I began to feel uneasy. Surely we would have reached the school and village by now. When I asked, the boy said he didn't know where we were. I had been riding for the last mile or so with my head chucked down into my coat collar to ward off the stinging snow from my face, but I had been guiding Bess to follow the boy who had again taken the lead. I could scarcely talk or move, I was so cold, but I knew Bess was heated from her exertion in the deep snow, going against the wind. I loosened the reins and gave her an encouraging "Go on, Bess." She at once pricked her ears and walked briskly away from the direction we had taken.

After what seemed an interminable time, I thought I could make out the forms of tepees near at hand. Now, houses. I put out my stiffened arm and felt—my barn! I heard the faint yap of Mazeppa indoors, and knew that we were safe. With difficulty we unsaddled the ponies and made them comfortable. Then we struggled to the house and built up the fires. The boy could not go back, so I made a bed for him in the schoolroom. We both drank much black coffee and ate bread and jelly. I rose early next morning to prepare breakfast for him, but he had gone back through the blinding blizzard which was still raging.

In due time I received a letter from my father:

We have been reading about the great blizzard in Dakota Territory. And that was the very day you started to the agency? What if you had been caught? Glad you came through safe. Do be careful about going far at this season of the year. . . . We had a little musical party last night— some fine music. . . . Mrs. Cleveland was at church. . . . Col Mac Allister died Saturday, sitting in a chair—was buried in Oak Hill Cemetery. . . . Yesterday your mamma made some salad and custard and other little fixings for Mrs. Ellis who is sick. Tomorrow that Mr. Ebbstrom of the picture-card firm proposes to bring a carriage around and take your mamma sight-seeing. Your mamma went to Mrs. Cleveland's reception last week—got terribly squeezed—was introduced to Mrs. Cleveland and the cabinet ladies—all very pleasant, etc. . . . You write about a partnership. There is always more or less danger in partnerships—especially for you. . . . If merits were confined to official achievement, I could pass a very creditable examination, but if I must be asked to state the height of the tallest tree in California, the greatest depth of the ocean, and the latitude of Timbuctu—and the retention of my place would depend on that—you can depend on it that I would be cut off. . . . Tell that old chief what's-his-name that his people *must* bring your wood and water and carry your messages and get your groceries without charge or you will go to another camp. . . . Your mamma and I are sending you a warm wrapper—I picked out the material and your mamma made it. . . . I went to church with Mr. Wilkerson, the new member, to the Pres. Church—he is a member—and the preacher spoke of all their church had done and mentioned many fine names. Then he said, "One little girl—a member of this church—

deserves special praise for unmarried, alone, and unprotected she has gone among untutored savages to the inclement climate of Dakota—She is a veritable female Caesar." Your mamma has presented me with a fine card table. . . . I hope you will stay in this weather. Be true to yourself and all obligations. Good night, little daughter.

Mr. Campbell had been adding to his herd of cattle, and now he came telling me that he thought himself wealthy enough to marry. I promised to marry him, but I was afraid to tell my people. I made plans for the wedding, though. I sent Mother fifty dollars with which she bought a very handsome piece of silk and a bonnet. She promised to make it to my order, and I, feeling both troubled and ungenerous, sat down and wrote both my thanks and my wedding plans in a long and dutiful letter.

The Fat Chief Shaska to Whom Corabelle Fellows Was
Alleged To Have Been Engaged

Corabelle Fellows' Fiance, Samuel C. Campbell

CHAPTER   SIXTEEN

I WAS much disturbed one day when a newspaper reporter from Chicago came to my door. Somehow the news had gotten abroad that I, a lady from Washington, was betrothed to a full-blood Indian chief. I was dumfounded and angry. The reporter went away. But that was just a beginning, for he went away to write a story of his own concoction which, I learned long afterwards, was copied far and wide. I was besieged constantly by men who knocked at the door of my schoolroom to get the latest slants on my romance. They went back and wrote even more disastrously what had already been so sadly miswritten. I refused them my photograph, and one of them obtained one from one of my pupils to whom I had given it. My fiancé had had no photograph. In lieu of his likeness one of these brilliant news scavengers hit upon the idea of taking the picture of a very old fat chief who sat for it for five dollars—as I learned long afterwards. He posed in his war regalia.

I was irritated, but I kept on with my usual routine, not dreaming that the fearful tale had traveled to Washington—had, in fact, gone from coast to coast—illustrated with a real photograph of myself and one of the fat old chief's. With hand trembling almost past using I tore uneven rips into a letter from home.

Their daughter's marrying an Indian was sufficient disgrace, but this cheap nation-wide publicity! With a torrent of words they attempted to forestall the proposed wedding. They sent almost daily telegrams to the agent, the minister of the little white church, and to myself. Not knowing what the newspapers were saying, and feeling that these superlatives were to be expected from Mother, I wrote back that I was very much in love, and went ahead with my plans. I had been gone from Washington just seven years. I set my wedding date for March 4, my birthday.

Twelve miles up the river stood the little white Episcopal church of my choice. It was served by an Englishman, a Mr. Hansford, who heard my story, met my fiancé, and approved my decision to go on with the wedding. March 4 the river was so jammed with ice that even the Indians would not attempt a trip by canoe. The wedding had to be postponed, anyway, because I had been unable to get to the post office at Forest City where my wedding dress from Washington was waiting to be delivered into my hands. I finally paid a messenger five dollars, and he brought the dress to me.

It was March 15 before we could make the trip to the church, March 15, 1888, and Friday. Dressed in our new clothes—my satin bonnet and gown were stylish, indeed, and Sam had a new tailor-made suit—we set out, hoping to arrive at the end of the twelve-mile drive by eleven. In our spring wagon lay the wedding cake I had baked for myself. Mrs. Hansford had insisted that she would bake the bride's cake, but I feared our postponement might have spoiled that desire, so I had baked one to make sure of so much. Ice still jammed and creaked in the river; snow lay heavily on the earth, but the sky was brilliant with a warming sun, and there was a crowd out to cheer us as we drove away.

As the snow melted the mud grew worse and worse. The winding road developed one mudhole after another. We slipped and slid up and down the interminable hills with greater and greater difficulty, until finally the wheels refused to turn.

Because of our wedding finery we wondered just what was to be done. At last Sam climbed down dismally to dislodge the mud from the wheels. Not more than five feet away stood a timber wolf. We had no weapons. Sam picked up a stone and hurled it with such good aim that the wolf ran off howling and did not return. It was a long weary time Sam spent tugging at the sunken wheels. Finally we got out of it and drove on, but our spirits were

sadly dashed. It was after three in the afternoon
when the little white church spire came in sight.

After a mud session in the woodshed and another
session with the wash basin, we went into the cold
little church and were married. Most of the Indian
guests who had come in the morning had grown
tired of waiting and gone away again. Still, we
had about a dozen guests. Happy, in spite of the
misadventures of the day, I cut my pyramidal
bride's cake, which was frosted in elaborate colored
designs, and enjoyed the tea which was to have
been a breakfast. We returned gaily as far as the
farm of Rebecca Holmes, where we were to spend
our three-day honeymoon. Rebecca Holmes, like
myself, was a schoolteacher who had married a man
with Indian blood.

Tuesday, when I reopened my school, I received
a shower. The children brought arrowheads, moccasins, food, and blankets. I was now nearer them
since I had married a man of Indian blood. Now I
was "Sister Blue Star." In grave curiosity the children looked Mr. Campbell over and named him
Mr. Blue Star!

School went on as usual until the mail began to
be flooded with offers of all kinds. Finally, since I
could see no reasons against going, we decided to
sign with a stereopticon bureau which was owned
by a Mr. Dewitt in Washington. We made quite
an extensive tour with him, speaking on Indians

Corabelle Fellows in Her Wedding Dress

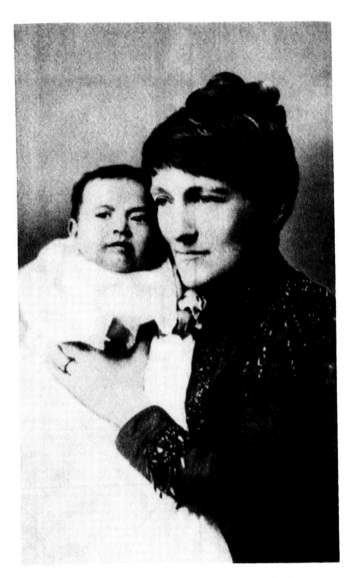

Corabelle Fellows and Her First Son, Chaské

and explaining his pictures. Later we made a second tour, the two tours covering most of the large cities of eastern and northern United States. With the handsome salary we thus earned we were able to stop off at Chicago on our return the last time and buy complete equipment and furnishings for the farm we had purchased. The second season we went again and returned with a fine saving.

On the first tour we had stopped in Washington. When I sent a messenger to the old home to say that I was in town, Father sent back a note saying Marian and Mother had gone to Atlantic City, but that he would come down to St. James Hotel to see us.

I had had no letters from home since my marriage. I knew what he meant. He found us waiting in the lobby.

"This is Mr. Campbell, my husband, Father," I said.

Poor Father! He looked up uncomprehendingly. The two men grasped each other's hands in a friendship that has lasted.

"Why—why—I had no idea, daughter," was as far as Father could get.

He looked at me strangely, then the old twinkle came into his eyes.

"Why didn't you tell me, daughter?" he said. Then the whole shocking story of the newspaper version of my marriage came out. Father fairly stammered in his haste to tell it. "I didn't think," he said, squeezing my hand until it hurt. "I didn't think—I couldn't actually believe that you would——"

"We are going to live on a farm," I broke in, tweaking his elbow, "a cattle ranch——"

And Father broke in with a bear hug and a smothering of kisses on my face, right there before everybody in the lobby of St. James Hotel.

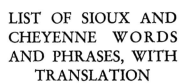

LIST OF SIOUX AND CHEYENNE WORDS AND PHRASES, WITH TRANSLATION

Note on pronunciation (from Riggs's *English-American Dictionary*)

Cheyenne: all sounds continental, except *ch*—sounded like the German gutteral.

Sioux: a, e, i, o, u—continental
c—aspirate like *ch* in chin
c—emphatic, vigorous
g—guttural like arabic *ghan*
h—guttural as in *kin*
n—italicized, nasal like French *bon*
q—like k
s—like *sh* in *shin*

SIOUX WORDS AND PHRASES

ahiti—to pitch a tent

ahi tipi—to come into camp

a hu ustan—I wish you would stop that

ake—again

amayaleso — where are you taking me?

asnipi—cured

ate (orateyapi)—father, superintendent, or governor

a wanicigal—I shall govern myself

a yu stan—they shall leave

blehemiciyo—I exert myself

ca—and

cahili — charcoal (or gunpowder)

can—wood, tree

can nonpa—wooden pipe

can silsilya—wild sage

can skata—play with wood (dominoes)

cante—heart

cante sica—your heart is bad (wood)

cezi—tongue

ecetu—it was fulfilled, or happened.

egle—placed
el—at
epinahan—I said
etan han—from
etipi—camped at
eyakas kapi—tied to it
eyanpahe—cried
eyo—say

galapi—go home
gemini—ten
glipi—they come back

hannedipi—God-seeking
    dream
he—this
he he—exclamation
hececa—thus
hege—thus he said
hekuys—come back
he miye—this is I
hena—these
he tue—whoever can this be?
higna—husband
hocoka—center of the holy
    circle
hopáke—a rawhide noose tied
    around horse's nose where a
    feather guided the beast
huh! takua cinstina—O gra-
    cious! she is too little!

icu—took
imaku wapi—spy upon me
ina—mother
inikaga—sweat lodge (purifi-
    cation)
inkpatáya—up-stream
iwan kam—above

iyatampi—to light a pipe in
    the sun
iyotiye wakiye—state or con-
    dition

kaga—made
kagapi—they made
kaska—to bind
katapila—my friends
key la—near
kin—the
ko—also
kola—friends
koskálaka—young men
kowokipi—fearful
kte lo—will be
kupi—they gave
ku wanna—came now
kuza—sick
kuzapi—were sick

lakas—certainly
leciya—hither
l'eyo—this he said
lila ota—knows much
lo—emphatic ending
lowan—to sing

mahpie acta—gone into the
    heavens
maka—earth
makahlilila—baked mud, clay
ma qu yi—give it to me
mastinchala—rabbit woman
maza zu—wad up
meneya—circle
mini—water
mitawa—mine
miye—myself

na—also, moreover
nacea—perhaps
nakenula—short time
nampa—two
napeche waka—nine
napemáyuxa—take my hand
napsiyohii—finger ring
napokatan—bracelet
nasula acta — no thinking with him (brainless)
natan hi wan—charge the enemy
nawazin—I stand
nicopi—they called you
nisi pela—commands me

ogle—shirts
ohinni—always
okicize—battle
olowan—songs
omani—travelers
onquon—where water was contained
opaquipi—filled
ota—many or much
oteliike—difficulty
owa—wrote or drew
owancaga—everywhere
owasin—all
owanzi—be quiet
oyakapo—tell it everywhere
Oyktehi—god of water
ozula—full

paslatipi—set up a tent
pezi—straw
piya—regenerate
piya wakag e—mad, insane
pté—little calf
pte ho—buffalo hide
pte hin ea ha — buffalo calf hide

qon—that

sayapi—they painted red
shadoan—eight
shakoin—seven
suka—thick
sunka—dog
sunka him tola—gray skinned dog
sunka wankan—horse (holy dog)

taku waste—how very good
takuskans—motion
temahilaqon—one who loves me dearly
tenkan—stone
tipic ina ya cin—would you care for turnip?
tiyata—at home
tokala—fix
toksu—travois
topa—four

unqonkt—we must separate

yahepapi—they drank all of it
yámini—three
yankape—stay in one place
yatkanpi—drank
yun kan—them

wacisa—baby
wakaje—I made
wakazin—travois
waksica—cup, bowl
wamii—one
wan—a
wanagi—soul (separate from body)
wan amikte—I am going away

wankan—holy
Wankan Tanka—the Great Mystery
wankanta—on high, above
wankici yaki—to see each other
wan maya kuwe—come to see me
wanna—now
wasena—pemmican
wasn—I am
wâsté—good
wasté sni—no good
watenkte—I shall eat
Watinyan—god of thunder
wawate—I am eating
welo—emphatic ending
wi—moon

wicasa—man
wicasa atawan oloman—man looking toward song
wicasi—told them
wichipitowan—blue star
wikcemna—ten
wikcemna tepo—forty
winyan—woman
wocé keya—prayer

yahepapi—drank
yamini—three
yankapo—stay in one place
yatkanpi—drank
yun kan—them
yunke lo—was killed
yutmkal—elsewhere

zaptan—five

Note—These words were edited by Edward Eagle Boy, a Sioux lad of seventeen attending American Indian Institute at Wichita, Kansas.

CHEYENNE WORDS AND PHRASES

ata—father
ayu!—how foolish!

chaska—first-born

dzinima—carrying bad word home

Ehani—our Father
el na ja wi—get up right now
etanioo—men

he tanu—sacred bow
hevisa—teeth
hiya!—call to dogs to go on
hitu—this one
honih hio—wolves
huchdjeho—wood-rats

imio missi yo—eating
ina—mother
inajan we—rise up
itaska winyn nasula—white-faced woman has no brains

kikilupi—get back!

le lela wasté—this is beautiful

ma achis—old man
mata—timber
meshivotzis—baby

napave—blessed
nama eyoni—holy men
nimadzi—carry

pi laya kia—my thanks I give
    you

siyo—many
stan yu—now you stop

tado un pejuta sapa—meat
    and black medicine-coffee
taeva—at night
taku shica achen—what bad
    thing is this?
taku wilakaikala—where are
    you going?

tanta—in sight
tsihotononihos—piled thick
tsiso—little one
tsitoni toyus—look
tsivais—those

ugh! can scotta hoksila—O,
    but you played on my child
    with long wood

vihnivo—on my way

Wakapola—Cut-Meat Creek

INDEX